THE
DEATH
OF
MEANING

The Death of Meaning

George V. Zito

PRAEGER

Westport, Connecticut
London

Library of Congress Cataloging-in-Publication Data

Zito, George V.
     The death of meaning / George V. Zito.
          p.   cm.
     Includes bibliographical references and index.
     ISBN 0–275–94674–6 (alk. paper)
     1. United States—Social conditions—1980–   2. Social change—
United States.   3. Meaning (Philosophy)   I. Title.
HN65.Z57   1993
306'.0973—dc20   93–15351

British Library Cataloguing in Publication Data is available.

Library of Congress Catalog Card Number: 93–15351
ISBN: 0–275–94674–6

First published in 1993

Praeger Publishers, 88 Post Road West, Westport, CT 06881
An imprint of Greenwood Publishing Group, Inc.

Printed in the United States of America

The paper used in this book complies with the
Permanent Paper Standard issued by the National
Information Standards Organization (Z39.48–1984).

10 9 8 7 6 5 4 3 2 1

Contents

Preface

Seventeen years ago I applied for a faculty position at a small, highly reputable Jesuit college in upstate New York. During the interview, the Sociology Department chairman, aware of my background, asked if I would consider teaching a course in population studies, an undergraduate version of my course in demography. I hesitated. "I could do that," I told him, "but you must understand that if I teach that course I will include the various methods of contraception and abortion, and I teach them from a positive standpoint: that is, I am *for* contraception, and I am *for* abortion (as long as it is not simply a redundant method of birth control but a choice of last resort). Will I get into any trouble with your administration or faculty if I teach such things?" The department chair, himself a Jesuit, shook his head. "No," he said, "you'll have complete academic freedom, of course. None of us will object. Parents of some students might object if they hear about it. But we will support you. You have the freedom to teach whatever your conscience dictates."

I was impressed. My maternal grandfather, the man in whose house I had grown up, had been very "anticlerical," and some of his feelings had rubbed off on me in my youth. Having fought in the Italian Unification, he was an antipapist who bemoaned Mussolini's conciliatory agreement with the Pope. He had always exhibited what I'd considered a healthy antifascist attitude, and the Jesuits, as I remembered them from my youth, were the "Pope's army" and if not fascists, then close to it. It was probably the lack of religious background resulting from my association with my grandfather that finally spurred my interest in religions, and resulted in some publications and conference presentations in the sociology of religion many years later. And resulted, too, in my having formed a lasting friendship with the Jesuit, the aforementioned chairman of that department.

I took the job. I taught the course the way I had said, and there were no grumblings anywhere. A year later I was offered a position at a large secular university with graduate as well as undergraduate programs, so I took that job and there I remain.

What brings the earlier incident to mind is an event that recently happened at this large secular institution. I was teaching an undergraduate course, Civilization and Society, that I had originated some years earlier under a foundation grant. The course includes a source book of readings from ancient Egyptian, Babylonian, Hebrew, Greek, Roman, Medieval and Renaissance authors. It is structured around the Durkheimian theses on the elementary forms of the religious life. Another shorter text explains different "systems" of social organization, not quite Parsonian, but including the Cultural System and the importance of values within that system. Many of the early readings reflect the religious orientations of their times, and one of the objects of the course is to show the development of a system of values within a civilization as well as the separation of the various institutional structures from the authoritarian charismatic person to the autonomy they have attained within modern bureaucratic social systems.

I had noticed that some of the student papers, when discussing the various gods and goddesses of the ancients, always omitted the *o* in the word *god*. "Zeus was a Greek g-d," I read. It did not take long before I realized that this occurred only with certain Jewish students. I tried explaining this in class one day. "Look," I said, "this has nothing whatever to do with the sacred name of the Hebrew god, Yahweh, which was considered ineffable— not to be written or spoken aloud—among orthodox Jews." I said that when I corrected papers written in English I expected

them to use good English. There was no course requirement
that they include the word *god* in any form in their papers for
my course, but if they did, they had better spell it correctly or
it would be marked wrong.

This created havoc. I received a call from the rabbi of the
campus Hillel organization, patiently explaining to me that there
was agreement among local congregations about the use of the
word *god* and that students are taught in their schools to omit
the letter *o* when they write *god* (with or without a capital letter).
"That's silly," I told him. "There is nothing special about that
English noun. Would they write "d-o" in Italian or "de-s" in
Latin? And what happens in German? Would they omit the first
or second *t* in *Gott*?" He did not appreciate my sense of humor.
"In my classes," I told him, "when students use English words
they must spell them correctly. If they don't, they are docked
for it, without exception." He objected loudly and vigorously. "I
am the professor and you are the rabbi," I told him. "You take
care of the religious well-being of your congregation and I will
teach them the secular stuff, and they'd better learn it correctly
or they are in trouble."

A few days later a Jewish professor who I did not know phoned
me and tried to rationalize the rabbi's position. "Tough," I told
him. "You and he are interfering with academic freedom here.
Either desist or I'll raise hell with AAUP and others. This was
all settled way back in the Scopes trial. No religious group is
going to dictate how I teach my science." That was the last I
heard from him, but not from the administration. A professor
in my own department, who has made a career out of being
Jewish, complained to the Affirmative Action or Human Resources person, who then tried to convince me that I should
tolerate this interference. "Nonsense," I told him. "I did not
leave a good position in engineering physics in the real world
to surrender my intellectual honesty in academia." When he
threatened to inform my dean, I told him he should go ahead
and do so.

And there the matter died. But I could not get over the in-
congruity here. Jews (and there are Jewish members of my own
family) were always the liberals fighting for freedom of expression, and the Jesuits were the dark secret army working against

social change, the conservatives or reactionaries. Somehow, the world had turned upside down in my lifetime. Christian fundamentalists of all varieties had always been the bad guys when I was growing up, and the Jews were always the good guys. What had happened?

The contradiction encouraged me to look with an even more jaundiced eye at what was happening about me. The scare tactics on campus with respect to rape (for example) had grown all out of proportion, and had resulted in separate camps of women and men not only among the faculty, but among the student body as well. Some groups of women talked about nothing else, and several committees and organizations had been formed to "educate" the rest of us on the matter of rape, as well as "sexual harassment." Something similar was happening within my own discipline. Women authors had stopped writing about sociology and were writing about "the patriarchical exploitation of women." That was *all* they were writing about, or most of them. The latest issue of *Contemporary Sociology,* the journal of book reviews published by the American Sociological Association, begins with a long listing of books on "gender." But these are all written by women. Do only women have genders? I mused. Who reads these books? Other women, I suppose. Books by men in sociology are read by both men and women, but not the "gender" books. This seemed to be on a par with the romance novels in the local drugstore. Harlequin Romances and their imitations are also only bought by women. Is there some connection here we have been missing? I know of no male colleague of mine who reads books of either of these genres. Is what Camille Paglia says true, that so-called Women's Studies is only institutionalized sexism, drowning our best women students in self-serving anti-intellectual pap?

These and similar musings soon led me to consider what these things must mean to their true believers. Because there are indeed true believers in this stuff. The advent of "political correctness" had suddenly made some of this stuff respectable, no matter how flawed it was in its reasoning or "empathetic feelings." Added to this, the subjectivism of postmodernism reduced all problems of meaning to antiepistemological trivia. I tried, in my classes, to explain to students at both levels that post-structuralism and postmodernism were not one and the same, and certainly not in sociology. Sociology had never had a distinctly "modernist" period such as that enjoyed by the Humanities, but we did have a "structuralist" period when Levi-Strauss leaned over from anthropology upon all the social sciences. "Postmodernism," from within a sociological perspective, is meaningless, I argued.

But then, I thought suddenly, most everything is getting meaningless these days. Is deconstructionism merely one aspect of a possible death of meaning? Is postmodernism? Political correctness? The abandonment of rigorous methodology in favor of gutsy hormonal response? What's been going on here? Why is the world becoming like a badly written imitation of a Kafka novel?

These are some of the disturbing sources of what follows. Almost everything I have written in my sociology career has had to do with meanings and language. Somehow these are now being threatened, and although it was difficult initially to define exactly where and how, and the point of it all, a modest amount of research yielded seemingly disproportionate results. These results are presented in the following chapters.

Chapter 1 ———————————

The Problem

The death of meaning: how can this be? Meanings change, have always changed, if what we mean by meaning is what we find in words, what words convey. The meaning of the word *jazz,* for example, changed from its origins as an off-color word for sexual coupling, to the kind of orgiastic dance signifying such behavior, to the music accompanying such a dance, to music without dance, to "all that jazz"—signifying nothing significant. Successive generations play with words, coin their own jargons to convince themselves that they are different from past generations, that "something is happening" and it's happening now, for them, the latest and the truest. That is nothing new. But meaning *itself* die? In the sense that meaning *itself* is disappearing? And not just the meanings of particular words? Can an argument be made for this seemingly outlandish idea? I believe it can. Most of us are aware that something of this sort has been happening for some time, but we haven't been able to put a finger on it. Nevertheless, in the series of essays that follow I hope to show that, although the death of God was announced early in the century and the death of Man midway through the century, both obituaries were misguided; here at the century's end it is clear that it is meaning that is disappearing—not just changing—that meaning itself is coming to an end, and in a certain way what

Nietzsche was talking about earlier and what Foucault[1] and others were talking about more recently is really the demise of meaning itself, both God and Man being manifestations of a deeper structure of language now in the process of decay.

In the course of the following essays we will examine various kinds of empirical evidence to suggest that what we unthinkingly refer to as "meaning" has been disappearing since early in the twentieth century. To understand what has been happening it will not be sufficient to merely give empirical examples of current situations, current activities: for at most these could be taken as signifying only a *change*, not the death, of meanings. And since we often (if mistakenly) assume that change is always positive and, therefore, that we are making progress as a society (as a nation, a group, or humanity itself), change is almost always welcomed. This well-known "myth of progress" has been attacked by philosophers and social theorists from Karl Marx through Karl Mannheim, by phenomenologists and existentialists alike, but it still persists, particularly among fervent disciples of popular ideologies. It will not be within the task of these essays to attempt to disprove once more the premise that any change is necessarily for the good, or represents progress: there are sources abundant for disproving that. To those emotionally committed to such a notion, however, all proofs are unconvincing, while to those who already understand, no further proof is required. This book is not intended for those who insist, like Candide, that all is for the best in the best of all possible worlds; it is intended for those who already have doubts about where we are going and why, although not (perhaps) so fervently imbued with the desire to believe that they can somehow stop the process—it appears that it has already gone too far for us to stop it—but to further understand it and somehow come to terms with it. Certainly, the collapse of the Soviet Union and the meaningless inter-ethnic savagery that resulted in the Balkans and elsewhere shows that the decline of meaning is not limited to the United States, but is endemic in the world. And there are, I am convinced, people in this world who feel quite passionately about attempting to understand the social construction within which they live and move and have their being and yet have had little if any hand in creating, in bringing into existence. The magnitude of this passion and the resulting confusion caused by the collapse of meaning only exacerbates their problem. By being born into a society and born into a language we become unwilling prisoners of language and society: it is not, necessarily, that such a thing as "free will" does not exist; but it has limits imposed by language and society that we often fail to take into account, particularly in sociology, psychology, and the other "human sciences." These limits serve contradictory ends: on the one hand, they impose restrictions on what may be said, written, published, or otherwise examined, as Foucault points out in his "Discourse on Language" and as Thomas Szasz, Ron Leifer and Ernest Becker discovered as early as 1962 in Syracuse when they challenged psychiatry's fictional claims to medical status.[2] On the other hand, these limits make possible the specification of meanings in verbal interactions between persons of the same language community by defining relations among and between related words. Words are defined by other words: that is what dictionaries are for. To master a language is to recognize the syntagmatic rules governing word order and the paradigmatic possibilities of meanings defined by the context in which they are used.

But is it possible to argue that meaning is dying, when the very process of conducting such an argument employs word language, the essential vehicle of meanings? When the words I use and the ways in which I use them have therefore themselves already undergone decay? I believe it is. Some contemporary French social discourses argue that we must restore to discourse its character as an event, while simultaneously maintaining that Man is dying during the event, also assuming this possibility. If we begin by recognizing the tentative nature of the communicative act and the attendant problem of intersubjectivity, the fact that we have taken some further steps down the ladder away from one-to-one mapping of meanings when we write or speak appears only as an additional historical impediment, another break in the possibility of full communication between us: it does not point to the impossibility of your understanding at least in part what it is I intend; it only suggests that communication between us has become increasingly difficult. That this condition is endemic in our world, and particularly in the United States, does not mean we must withdraw into isolated shells and abandon all attempts at communication.

Death being a more permanent condition than mere change, we must be shown examples of some current conditions that would lead one to conclude that meaning itself is dying, rather than the meanings of particular words changing. Because of the complexity of the situation, some seemingly complicated examples may be given before others more simple, to help us grasp the multifaceted process that is underway. For now we need only notice the continuing shift away from words to pictures (or icons) and reflect that although word systems—languages—are the most complex meaning systems, systems of signs, that we have for communication of complex ideas and discourses, television has largely replaced printed text as the principal source of information and knowledge for most Americans. Demotic language evolved originally *away* from picture languages such as hieroglyphics, and not the other way around. Our current historical movement from demotic language to pictures is therefore a reversal of a long historical process that had prevailed throughout the various cultures of the West.

Many of us have seen in our lifetimes word language media such as newspapers, magazines, and books steadily declining in availability. How many newspapers existed in major American cities fifty years ago? In New York City alone, where are the *Herald Tribune, The Sun,* the *World Telegram,* the *New York Journal* and the *Journal American*? Whatever happened to the *New York Mirror*? *PM*? Where are the print media of yesteryear? With books the matter is much the same. At times young listeners are shocked when I describe the Fourth Avenue Booksellers that existed in New York when I was young: "how could they disappear?" they ask. That logocentricity has declined is always a revelation to them. Today, in New York City, for example, not only bookstores like Brentano's have disappeared but the quasi-scholarly bookstores as well. Dial Books is gone, the Eighth Street bookstores are replaced with fast-food eateries; only Strand and a few others remain. In smaller cities, even university towns, the situation is not much different. The colleges' own bookstores remain to furnish textbooks for courses, although they have mostly (like Harvard's Co-op) become oversized department

stores with a dwindling emphasis upon scholarly books. Even
the independent, book-lovers' bookstores and the people who
operated them, the informal literary mentors of the emerging
tastes of many of us still alive, those book dealers who knew
books, lived books, breathed books, and socialized several generations to books, have all but disappeared.

The situation is somewhat better in Toronto and other parts
of Canada—where literate populations still exist and where it
is still possible to buy serious books—but in the United States,
even in college towns like Ithaca and Syracuse, Madison and
Ann Arbor, most literate book dealers have abandoned all hope
as we drive further into a future of iconic receptiveness, in
which various varieties of video represent major components.
Video rentals have replaced the book rentals of the earlier
years; the public libraries have increasingly become the place
to borrow free videos rather than free books. In the United
States, Boston is among the last to go. Illiteracy in the United
States is now higher than in any other Western society and
SAT scores, which show students' ability to read and understand the meanings of questions and verbal examples, have
dramatically declined; Hirsch's book is only one of many re-
countings of some of the implications.[3]

The German sociologist Georg Simmel, early in the century[4]
discussed what he called "the web of associations" within which
individuals were embedded in modern societies, and called particular attention to certain social forms[5] that are elemental. Such
forms as the dyad and the triad (i.e., groups of two and three)
he saw as including bonds between and among individuals of a
social kind, and typify the "forms of sociation"[6] that have arisen
to serve human life by fostering interaction among individuals,
and as a consequence of such interaction making society itself
possible. Taken together, such forms constitute an intricate web
of connecting links among such individuals, often uniting them
into communities of common interests, where the obligations to
others are recognized and accepted despite the pluralism that
may exist due to differences in cultural backgrounds and personal interests. For Emile Durkheim, the greatest French sociologist, this "web" took the form of a "collective conscience," a
kind of group morality where social norms, expectations of what

one ought to do or ought not to do with respect to others, acted as *social facts* and influenced one's actions, although not in a straightforward stimulus-response manner. A social fact for Durkheim meant anything external to the individual that exerted a coercive effect on the individual's behavior. Other social theorists held similar beliefs in their attempts to respond to the age-old questions posed by the philosopher Thomas Hobbes: "How is society possible? Why isn't there a war of all against all?" Somehow people *did* cooperate socially by living in communities and sharing moral and ethical standards, and society, that web of associations among people which existed before they did, continued to exist when they had passed through it and other people had replaced them. There were changes, of course, brought about by the discovery of America, the French Revolution, the Industrial Revolution. Most social scientists concerned with the historical dimension are quick to point out how world views changed with time: the Great Chain of Being of the Medieval world gave way to the decentered world of Copernicus and then later to Western capitalism, to urbanization and industrialization, to different understandings of the place of religion, of men and women; adolescence came into existence as an intermediary stage in personal development. The old cry of "Liberty, Equality, and Fraternity" got written into laws. Equal justice under the law was given new life and persisted as a universal demand upon government.

But increasingly, in the latter half of the twentieth century, the earlier meaning of "liberty" became simplified and equated with personal "rights." "Equality" changed in meaning to "sameness," and "fraternity" disappeared altogether, suddenly seen as an anachronism of a more revolutionary era and vaguely suspected of being associated with "patriarchy." By fraternity was meant community; but community, except in small ethnic enclaves in ghettos and barrios, had all but disappeared from the American scene. Community, Durkheim had argued, is only possible where there is a collective conscience and social interaction, where citizens share common bonds and interests and increase the "moral density" of an area—not the physical density necessarily but the density of mind and of number and kinds of interactions.[7] In this sense college fraternities and sororities are atavistic remnants of an association closer to that of the bonds of blood relations of preindustrial societies than to (for example) the political parties or ideological movements of contemporary America. Durkheim was disturbed by the disappearance of such bonds, and dreamed of a day when the work and professional groups characterizing industrial society would themselves generate social bonding and make a new form of social integration possible. Like Marx's dream of the triumph of the proletariat, the new society never arrived. For Max Weber, the greatest of the German social theorists, Western rationality concealed the irrational base Nietzsche had so clearly seen, and the consequence of the pursuit of this rationality could lead only to the imprisonment of Western man in an isolated cage of his own creation.

Increasingly, in the latter half of this century, we have seen a decrease in social interaction and in group participation in collective actions of all kinds except the destructive. Democratic voting has declined and marriage and family activity decreased, while warfare and other forms of slaughter have increased. What we have witnessed too is the decline of Simmel's triads and dyads and the emergence of what can only be referred to as the monads, single social units, individuals incapable or unwilling or unable to form a bond to at least one other person, let alone to engage in social bonding of any form. Their inability to form what they mistakenly call "meaningful relationships"—mistakenly because all relationships are by definition meaningful—has had significant effects not only on the formation of families, but on increased antagonisms between the sexes, the races, the religious bodies, exacerbating the separation of individuals and further precluding the establishment of integrative social bonds. Their lives are characterized by a general isolation from all forms of community, and they often immerse themselves either in work or in ritualized barroom "fun" to escape the vacuity of an otherwise empty existence. The "yuppy" was only one variety of this species. This emerging class was eagerly seized upon by purveyors of athletic equipment, electronics manufacturers, and other entrepreneurs anxious to take advantage of the new business opportunities afforded by this isolation of the individual from all social bonds. Take the lonely jogger, for example. Removed from companionship and insulated from the social world around him or her by the earphoned Walkman, this lonely runner is condemned to a food regimen dictated by quasi-scientific prophets descending from Capitol Hill in Washington (the bearded Surgeon *General* in his *naval* uniform) or from the health and food commentator of the local TV station. Not only frozen to an impotence of choice among foods for fear of carcinogens, cholesterol, fats of all kinds (substituting frozen yogurt for ice cream, oat bran for cereal, and skim milk for whole milk), he or she lives in fear of radon in the cellar, foam insulation in the walls, chemical fertilizers on the lawn, and secondary cigarette smoke, which contaminate the vestal purity of the lungs. Looking up, in a kind of Consumer's Union Guide to Physical Immortality, what he or she should be eating, thinking, doing next— the lonely earphoned, Walkmanned runner is the symbolic embodiment of the death of meaning: unable, for lack of socialization into the family of humanity, to consult what David Riesman long ago referred to as an "inner gyroscope" to furnish guidance[8] for his or her own actions. This person is condemned to rely upon external, specious and self-proclaimed "authorities" (the entertainment media as well as the State) to steer a course in life.

How did this come about? Why do marriage rates fall, divorce rates increase? Sociologists, following the classical theoretical insights of Durkheim, Marx, Weber, Simmel and the other masters of the social sciences, would not claim that suddenly everybody decided that "this was the thing to do." For Durkheim, especially, the doubt was particularly acute.[9] Whenever we find a collective phenomenon explained on the basis of individual psychologies, he argued, we can be sure the explanation is false. We must search within the society for social explanations. We must find some kind of social fact operating on the collectivity that could explain why, for example, Hungarians have higher suicide rates than the Irish, the Irish have higher alcoholism rates than the Italians, and so forth. In other words, we must explain collective activities in terms of collective properties, not individual properties. Similarly, to understand the present state of American society it makes no sense to say that "people decided that they wanted to do such and such" or "women decided that from now on" or "men just agreed to give in." Such pop explanations miss the point and explain nothing at all. They are as pointless as applying a crude Marxist explanation—that exploitation is implicit in the relations to production—or more simplistically, to blame "The Bosses," Wall Street and Madison Avenue.

Such explanation is unsatisfactory from a sociological as well as a humanistic viewpoint. We must search beyond such pop "explanations" and ideological rhetorics to the underlying system of meanings, structures, and relations within which we are embedded. We must explore the web of associations, the very fabric of what we mean by society and social life.

Thus, we begin, in this book, by examining certain widespread phenomena we otherwise might ignore. We shall tread certain paths some classical and some not-so-classical thinkers have suggested, and extrapolate from them to inform our present situation. Christopher Lasch, Richard Sennett, Michel Foucault, and certain other modern and postmodern theorists have already made significant inroads in this direction. I will employ some classical theoretical perspectives with theirs, with a view toward understanding the ongoing process. Since this discussion is not limited to social scientists, I will not assume the readers' familiarity with the classical sources. For those with backgrounds in the social sciences generally, and in sociology in particular, the sources should be familiar, although my use of them may not be. The work of Georg Simmel complements the Durkheim-Mauss thesis, *Primitive Classification*: if "the classification of things follows the classification of men," which is what Durkheim and his nephew claimed, then this applies to social forms generally.[10] In other words, we impose upon all reality those sets of relations we find within the human family. As families have hierarchical structures, so we have imposed hierarchical structures on all our scientific and social cognitions. We speak of the "*mother* lode," and we arrange the natural elements in the periodic tables of our knowledge and discourse. Radon is, after all a "*daughter* element" of radium, for example. Some elements belong to the halogen *family*, while others belong to other families. As each of us has a beginning, and an end, so must everything in our cognitive field have a beginning, and an end. Radioactive elements have "half *lives*." More than metaphor is involved here. The transmission of specific meanings, relative to the natural objects described, depends upon these concepts borrowed from the relations among human individuals. Durkheim and Mauss were eager to show that the social, the set of relations uniting individuals, is the primary source of our understanding of the world. "There is no meaning where the classifications of social life are gone," Mary Douglas reminds us.[11] To act we require a certain certainty, or inner assurance, that what we do will have the desired outcome. We want our actions to be met with consequences dictated by our cultural expectations, by what we have come to believe is "normal" and usual in the world about us. But, having immersed ourselves in a behaviorist and Freudian psychological dualism, we claim to know more than we can know and become latter-day impotent Hamlets, who see too many sides of the situation but no one side clearly enough to predicate action upon it. Unlike Hamlet, however, we are not part of an ontological unity, a world view of inner consistency where normative expectations have retained sufficient coercive power upon human action to make a "collective conscience" possible. That certain inner assurance has been depleted, and we are characterized most often by our uncertainties. Hamlet could be so shocked by the action of others that he insisted upon writing in his book, "A man may smile, and smile, and be a villain." We, however, not only take this insight for granted but admire a smiling video J. R. in the pot-boiler TV serial *Dallas* for being such a villain. Indeed, we may amorally, or immorally, take certain satisfactions in our own villainies, although our skill in furnishing accounts[12] or rationalizing our behavior assures us that we do no more than our victims would do, the opportunity presenting itself. Certain fields within sociology, such as ethnomethodology and symbolic interactionism, offer us clues to the mechanisms of the process[13] and the advances into the poststructuralism of Foucault and others allow us to examine discourses as ways of penetrating the constraints upon our understanding. I have explored elsewhere some transformations permitting redactions of known truisms or orthodoxies into other nomenclatures and vocabularies[14] but these will be touched upon again, as well as certain aspects of discourse, such as defusing, in which we can discern the changes in the linguistic activity within which meanings are encoded.

Finally, we shall have recourse to a wealth of empirical materials that will serve as examples of the malaise we are examining.

The following essays may not be in an ideal narrative order. Indeed, the very notion of such an ideal narrative order has become increasingly problematic. As meanings decline, so too does the concept of order and our understanding of what properly constitutes a text or a narrative. In the "postmodern" world[15] texts are increasingly "deconstructed"[16] to mean whatever the reader wishes them to mean to satisfy his or her own glandular or ideological cravings, a thing William Faulkner warned us against in his Nobel Prize acceptance speech. Deconstruction is one other assault upon the status of meanings. This presents a problem for authors, not readers: in striving to be clear, so as not to be "misunderstood" an author is aware that his intentions may become irrelevant to a deconstructionist reader, and the organization of a text becomes a problem. In the following, each chapter may be read as an essay in itself; taken together, however, and positioned as they are between this introduction and the closing chapter, they constitute an attempt to explicate the malaise of American society at the end of the twentieth century: a period in which we have suffered the national embarrassment of a grade-B movie actor cast in the role of president of the United States (and often forgetting his lines)[17] followed by a new vice president of doubtful intelligence and proven incompetence, together with a companion in office, George Bush, who was elected by the lowest percentage of eligible voters of any president in history and who waged his own variety of warfare, killing imagined enemies by the thousands in Panama and Iraq; a time when a Los Angeles jury shocked the world by failing to find the police officers guilty in the widely observed video of the barbaric beating of a black citizen; a time when a consumption model was foisted upon American universities by a new business-oriented administration that considers itself management and faculty members as mere employees, students as consumers of a product, placing money above mind in its scale of values; when strike-breaking activities of the national government became widespread and inspired scab labor as the norm, rather than the exception to the norm, and destroyed the last vestige of populist community; where poverty annually increases, illiteracy flourishes, and our infant mortality rates stand out among the family of Western nations; where women increasingly attack not only men, but the very notion of maleness, transforming even the "Father in heaven" into a female functionary; where males and females, blacks and whites, Jews, Gentiles, and Moslems, young and old, grow increasingly antagonistic to each other. A time, in short, where individuals suffer not only from "identity crises," but where the meaning of identity itself and the notion of a person has become such an onerous burden that the very idea of society in the formation of a "self" becomes insignificant and suffocates an individual's attempt to reach out to another for any other purpose than the instantaneous gratification of personal erotic or egotistical needs: where history is seen as irrelevant to the Now and hence is either forgotten or ignored; when vocabularies become depleted and the possibility of adult communication lost, the infantile and teenage verbal incompetence prized; where everyone has his or her "right" to his or her special "thing," whatever that thing may be. And where whatever it is that is designated as a "right" is as devoid of meaning as one's life purpose itself, crude will in all its stubborn antipathy relegating ethical and moral considerations to the trash barrels of Macintosh iconography.

How did it come about that we Americans, starting out on a long heralded journey to the promised land, have arrived instead at this dark and lonely place? That is the problem and the situation these essays confront.

NOTES

1. Foucault's "death of man" thesis and his restoration of discourse as an event is best explored in his *The Archaeology of Knowledge,* particularly in the Appendix, "Discourse on Language"; see Michel Foucault, *The Archaeology of Knowledge* (New York: Harper and Row), 1972. See also, in this connection, Charles Lemert. *Sociology and the Twilight of Man.* Carbondale, Ill.: Southern Illinois University Press, 1979; and Jacques Derrida, *Of Grammatology,* Baltimore, Johns Hopkins University Press, 1976. For a discussion of the myth of progress, see Robert Nisbet, *History of the Idea of Progress* (New York: Basic Books), 1980.

2. Thomas Szasz is the author of the well-known book, *The Myth of Mental Illness*; and Ernest Becker of the Pulitzer Prize-winning book,

The Denial of Death. Ron Leifer's book, *In The Name of Mental Health: The Social Functions of Psychiatry* is one of several books exposing the myths of psychiatry and its abuses as an agent of social control. All three authors suffered at the hands of institutionalized medicine. "Becker (had) refused to go to the State Hospital on the grounds that he was employed by the medical school, not the State Hospital. The State Hospital had renounced the principle of academic freedom when it barred his colleague, Dr. Szasz, from teaching there. Becker said he was willing to meet with (Dr. Marc) Hollender at the medical school. Hollender fired Becker on the spot. Becker won a Pulitzer Prize in 1974 for his masterful work, *The Denial of Death.*

"I was fired in 1966 by Hollender's hand picked successor, Dr. David Robinson. . . . One day, in the midst of a dispute about whether Dr. Stanley Diamond and Ernest Becker—then of the Department of Anthropology at Syracuse University—should be brought in as guest lecturers, Robinson burst into my office and announced that he was not going to renew my appointment. In academic parlance, this meant I was fired. . . . Robinson told me he was firing me because he did not want my book published while I was in the department. He was afraid that between Szasz and me the department would lose NIMH money and prospective residents. . . . Dr. Becker and I were vulnerable because we did not have tenure. What happened to Szasz, Becker and me is important for more than our own personal interests and careers.

"Above all it is important to the increasing number of victims of psychiatric abuse. Society has given psychiatry the power to confine people against their will and force drugs and electroshock on them. This is the issue Szasz raised and this is the issue which was repressed at Syracuse in 1963 and is continuing to be repressed by the psychiatric establishment today.

"The events at Syracuse are important because they were the beginning of a continuing effort by establishment psychiatry to repress and silence its critics. . . . The events at Syracuse have profound implications for academic and intellectual freedom in this country. Psychiatry pretends to be a science, but it serves social and political functions disguised as medical treatment. The American public is being fed false claims about mental illness by a profession that functions as a covert form of social control, which has pecuniary interest in denying and disguising this role and defining itself as medical and which represses and ignores its critics." From an article, "Psychiatry Prohibits Debate," by Dr. Ron Leifer in the Syracuse, *Post Standard,* March 26, 1992, in response to an article appearing earlier about the Szasz incident.

3. E. D. Hirsch, Jr., *Cultural Literacy: What Every American Needs To Know* (Boston: Houghton Mifflin), 1987.

4. Some of the best of Simmel's work is included in translation in Donald Levine's book *Georg Simmel: On Sociability and Social Forms* (Chicago: University of Chicago Press), 1971.

5. By social forms Simmel was referring to such things as superordination and subordination, friendship, love, secrecy, and other interactional phenomena characterizing the exchanges between persons.

6. Sociation is the term most often used in English translations in explicating Simmel's forms. See Donald Levine's introduction in *Simmel*, 1971.

7. Moral density, too, is a term of Durkheimian sociology; the concentration and variety of mental activity at a location, rather than simply the number of persons at that same location, is what Durkheim was attempting to specify.

8. David Riesman, Nathan Glazer, and Reuel Denny, *The Lonely Crowd: A Study in the Changing American Character* (New Haven: Yale University Press), 1950.

9. Emile Durkheim, *Rules of the Sociological Method* (New York: Free Press), 1938.

10. Emile Durkheim and Marcel Mauss, *Primitive Classification* (Chicago: University of Chicago Press), 1963.

11. Mary Douglas, *Implicit Meanings* (London: Routledge and Kegan Paul), 1975, p. 247.

12. See Stanford Lyman and Marvin Scott, "Accounts," *American Sociological Review* 33, pp. 46–63.

13. See, for example, Harold Garfinkle, *Studies in Ethnomethodology* (Englewood Cliffs, N.J.: Prentice-Hall), 1967.

14. George V. Zito, *Systems of Discourse: Structures and Semiotics in the Social Sciences* (Westport, Conn.: Greenwood Press), 1984.

15. For a definition of postmodernism, see Jean-François Lyotard, *The Postmodern Condition* (Manchester: Manchester University Press), 1984. For a general introduction and discussion of developments, see Steven Connor, *Postmodern Culture: An Introduction to Theories of the Contemporary* (Oxford: Basil Blackwell), 1989.

16. Jacques Derrida, 1976. The popularity of such destructive "deconstruction" among American feminist writers has prompted the structuralist linguist Julia Kristeva to rename it "condestruction" (i.e., cunt-destruction) in her French language novel, *Les Samourais, romans*.

17. The record of Reaganisms is best delineated by Paul Slansky in his book, *The Clothes Have No Emperor: A Chronicle of the American 80s* (New York: Simon and Schuster), 1989.

Chapter 2 _____

The Demise of Holidays

A slow process has been underway in American society that until now has gone largely unnoticed. It has not been an overnight transition but has slowly and surreptitiously crept into well-established institutional forms. It has had many disparate facets, invading so many aspects of society that each facet, by itself, did not appear significant at the time it emerged. Pieced together in historical perspective, however, these seemingly unconnected events constitute an historical phenomenon of unprecedented magnitude.

The death of meaning first became evident in the United States in the routinization and demystification of holidays. Holidays had been traditionally associated with specific assigned calendar dates or the occurrence of certain days of the week: Labor Day on the first Monday of September, Christmas on the 25th of December, Washington's birthday on the 22nd and Lincoln's on the 12th of February, and so on. Holidays were celebrated on the days they commemorated. A holi*day* signified a special day, giving to the celebrated day a festive or solemn air, according to the nature and meaning of the commemorated event. The eleventh hour of the eleventh day of the eleventh month was a special solemn moment, torn out of history by the end of a cataclysmic world-wide catastrophe, World War I. Thanksgiving was a feast day of national significance, commemorating the pilgrims' survival of their first winter in the New World. It was a time when families, their members widely separated by the geographic dispersion of the population so prevalent in America, got together for a feast of traditional foods. For many immigrants it was a day to offer a special prayer of thankfulness for the bounty they had found in America. Independence Day, the Fourth of July, was a day to celebrate the success of the American Revolution and independence from England. Fireworks and home-town parades marked the special occasion. It was the day of our national identity.

For the past fifteen or twenty years, however, special significance has been removed from particular holidays: the Fourth of July, for example, is no longer celebrated *on* the Fourth of July, unless it happens to fall on a Monday. Other holidays have been similarly adjusted so that they make possible "long weekends" (i.e., Saturday through Monday vacations). Although this may boost tourism and simplify industrial and business schedules, further "rationalizing" bureaucratic procedures, it effectively removes from the day any unique celebratory significance: the day becomes one more occasion for a long weekend. Any ritualistic specificity is accordingly lost. The "Monday off" becomes the central meaning of the day. Since all such holidays now result in "Mondays off," differences between holidays (for example whether we celebrate Thanksgiving or the Fourth of July) become irrelevant and are at last forgotten. The name of the holiday persists but the meanings associated with it are absent and no longer significant. Thus, the differences among and between holidays and the meanings such differences once designated are now lost, except for a few "traditionalists" outside the mainstream of contemporary American life. Holidays that are truly religious *holy days* (as the word originally implied) have remained impervious to such changes; they originated prior to the creation of the United States and were sedimented in church calendars. The government and the retail industry have hesitated to challenge their designation. Christmas *must* be the twenty-fifth of December: it is protected by the threat of sacrilege and the power of the established western Christian churches. Similarly, Easter *must* be the first Sunday after the first full moon following the vernal equinox.[1] So ordained by the doctors of the Church, secular efforts at change would be seriously resisted and condemned.

All matters pertaining to the celebration of holidays had historically been a property of civil society. In exercising its political authority upon the calendar, making the holiday significant only as the occasion for another long weekend, the State has crystallized its marriage to its economic establishment and further increased its domination of civil society.

It may be deemed significant that the British use the word *holiday* much as the Americans use *vacation*. "He is on holiday," the British say, meaning that he is off from work for a rest. However, the American use of the word *vacation* means something more than this, and is closer in meaning to its root, evident in words such as *vacate*: it involves not merely resting, but going off somewhere. If one remains at home, this is not a "vacation." Moreover, as any American visitor to Canada (for example) is at once aware, if he or she visits Toronto or Montreal on Good Friday, a holiday in Canada, one will be shocked to find not only banks but stores of all kinds closed for the day. But Good Friday is not an occasion for closing businesses or stores in the United States; indeed, in most states, stores feature special sales on "holidays" to attract the shoppers who, having the day off (and perhaps unable to avail themselves of the pleasures promised them by the State in its offer of redundant long weekends), will go to the shopping malls for lack of anything better to do. The only holiday on which most American retail businesses close is Christmas; not Good Friday, Easter, the Fourth of July, or any other holiday, and this day only because of the possible protest of their employees. They compensate for the loss of business on this day by decorating their stores much earlier and inviting Santa Claus on Thanksgiving. For many years retailers, through their advertising and promotions, had made the days from Thanksgiving to Christmas Eve *the* shopping season for the year: indeed, as a preliminary step in the destruction of the meaning of Thanksgiving, Macy's department store had Santa Claus arrive at the end of its Thanksgiving Day parade, signaling the onset of the shopping season assault on consumers by the department stores. More recently, department-store Christmas decorations precede even Thanksgiving Day, with Santas replacing turkeys as the symbolic icons. Thanksgiving itself still occurs on a Thursday, but the designation of the specific Thursday varies from year to year at the whim of the national government. And for many Americans it is no longer celebrated as a holiday at all.

This manipulation of the dates of holidays to foster the demands of the market, rather than the national, religious, or historical significance such holidays previously embodied, does more than merely increase the power of the State over civil society: it makes the meanings associated with these holidays completely irrelevant. The bond that previously existed between the individuals in the society and the heroes, real or imaginary, of the cultural inheritance is subverted. Many Americans still alive remember that Lincoln's birthday was celebrated on the twelfth of February, Washington's on the twenty-second. But the newer "Presidents' Day," that has replaced both birthdays in fact celebrates neither: it simply creates a long weekend, for many useless at that time of year and for all no longer associated with either president. At most, it is a day of "white sales" by retail establishments. Thus, an integrative social bond to the past and its heroes has been broken. If, as often claimed, American school children no longer have a sense of history, American or otherwise, and are obsessed with the valueless and nondirective Now, the manipulation of the calendar by the State away from historical interests in favor of the interests of business must share some of the blame for the children's ignorance. In this transition the meanings associated with holidays have been lost; but more significantly, an attack has been launched on the status of meaning itself. By making each holiday no different from any other holiday the relations among holidays—what makes Easter something separate and distinct from Labor Day (for example) and having little to do with the calendar in and of itself—meaning has been subtracted, not merely substituted. The leveling-off of the holiday process to equal status for all holidays—whether they once commemorated the crucifixion of Christ or the end of a disasterous war—removes the unique emotional and cathectical content from the *event* itself as it does from the *day* itself. A holiday becomes one more occasion to serve tourism or the retail industry. While there has been a *change* in meaning here, it should be clear that meaning itself has suffered a blow. By erasing differences, relations among targets of cognition become at first blurred and then disappear. A thing is what it is, after all, to the extent that it differs from other things, that it has a unique stamp of its own. And in the absence of such differences among the elements of our understanding, there can be no such things as meanings. From Alfred North Whitehead through Ferdinand de Saussure[2] and the later disciples of both, it is clear that meanings lie not in things themselves, in their "essences," so called, but in the relations among such things. Whitehead put the matter most clearly: "The misconception which has haunted philosophy throughout the centuries is the notion of 'independent existence.' There *is no such mode of existence.* Every entity is to be understood in terms of the way it is interwoven with the rest. . . . the event is what it is by reason of the unification within itself of a multiplicity of relations. Outside this system of relations, it is nothing." This applies to all things: women, flags, pencils, and each and every other target of cognition, objective or psychological, including holidays. By removing the multiplicity of relations characterizing a holiday, its interweaving with other things, its embeddedness in the relations of historical events, the holiday as holiday ceases to exist. Its meaning has died. And in its death, it kills an integral part of meaning itself.

NOTES

1. Although the designations for Christmas and Easter vary with different calendars employed by different Christian communities, in the United States even those observing Eastern Rite designations participate on 25 December when it comes to civic or national events associated with the holiday.

2. Ferdinand de Saussure, *Course in General Linguistics* (New York: McGraw-Hill), 1959.

Chapter 3

Applause! Applause! The Routinization of Ritual

The manipulation of holidays by government is only one activity of many that has led to the gradual decline and ultimate death of meaning. There are other activities, performed not only by governments but unknowingly by the public at large, that contribute their share to the demise. The routinization of certain ritual performances is an example of this.

What is referred to here as the *routinization* of a social activity is a process that provides the activity with a measure of predictability based upon both its regulation and its subsequent confinement to a redundant format. It is in part this element of redundancy in the transformation of holidays into long weekends that constitutes the routinization of holidays in American society. But it is only one small step in the destruction of meaning. Routinization minimizes claims to uniqueness and subsumes the occasion or practice within some well-established social form. Max Weber's discussion of the routinization of charisma is perhaps the best known example.[1] Since charisma is an innate personal property, ascribed rather than achieved, and lends to the possessor the power of authority and leadership, the transmission of such power to possible successors becomes a problem. Charisma, as such, cannot be transmitted unless the successor is similarly blessed with this special characteristic of personality.

This was quite evident in our own time, when the death of the charismatic Martin Luther King, Jr., resulted in the ascension of Ralph Abernathy to the leadership of the Southern Christian Leadership Conference. Abernathy was an ordinary man who, like most of us, lacked charisma, and as a consequence the movement for civil rights faltered. According to Weber, Western societies evolved bureaucratic structures to guarantee the transmission of leadership and authority, thus obviating the need for charisma. Authority became vested in office, rather than in the person, and qualifications for office were then established. Thus a routinization process enabled bureaucratic organizations, in government and business, to continue to exist in spite of the corrupt personages that might at times occupy the office. It is clear from Weber's discussion that religious leadership itself, and many activities and practices of a similar kind, are also subject to routinization. It is perhaps less clear whether nonreligious or secular activities follow the same processes of routinization as the religious. Charisma is, after all, essentially a religious phenomenon. However, just as secular heresies are produced by the decline of religious monopolizations[2] and the increase in secularization[3] as a consequence of transformations occurring in discourse,[4] we may reasonably expect that whatever secular practices exist having religious or quasi-religious features may undergo similar processes.[5] This seems to have occurred not only with respect to businesses, but also with respect to holidays. Other patriotic, militaristic, and nationalistic ceremonies often share religious features. There are rituals (such as saluting the flag, e.g.) that foster group solidarity and social integration and serve to bind one into a community of believers where one shares meanings with other participants.[6] The significance of secular no less than religious rituals is central to the theoretical concerns of the great French sociologist Emile Durkheim and his commentators.[7]

Secular rituals are familiar to us all; they are frequently defined as "rites of passage"[8] among the young and those in professional careers: the ceremonial practice of being granted academic tenure and promotions (for example), the issuing of a driver's license for the first time, initiation into a fraternity or sorority, beer drinking parties among college students, and so forth. These all point to the group-binding communal feature of ritual at some level of understanding and are secular in nature.

The matter of social integration is complex, and is not our immediate concern. Instead, my objective is twofold: first, to call attention to a particular transformation that has been occurring among some forms of secular ritualistic behaviors and to speculate on its origin; and second, to provide examples of the processes through which the latent meanings provided by such rituals are being eliminated. I stress the aspect of speculation as to the origin of the transformation, since both the nature of the phenomenon and available methods of investigation preclude a "more positive" assertion. Most of the following examples are drawn from political contexts because the political is the most familiar setting for secular rituals. However, as already mentioned, there are other secular contexts, such as the educational, fraternal, business, and indeed all social activities where ritual or ritualistic behaviors play significant parts.

The following discussion employs examples of ritualistic behaviors based on controlled observations and interviews conducted over the period 1986 through 1992.

The playing and singing of national anthems is widespread among Western populations, and its ongoing transformation in the United States provides a convenient place to start. The British "God Save the Queen (or King)" is perhaps the most widely distributed national anthem because of the earlier extent of the British Empire. In the 1930s a version of this anthem ("My Country 'Tis of Thee") was replaced in the United States by "The Star Spangled Banner." This is played and sung at collective gatherings, where group identification and group solidarity are fostered, with a display of the flag. From a Durkheimian standpoint, it would seem that the purpose of such a ritual is to remind the many individuals present, who may otherwise be strangers to each other, of their common national bond.

Although group singing of national anthems may have enhanced the feelings of common identity among participants in such communal rituals, it later became a general practice in the United States to have a professional singer lead the singing. Having a leader had the effect, particularly at events involving large crowds, of discouraging group singing of the admittedly

difficult melody in favor of the professional singer's performance. The only persistent unifying bond existed in the act of
rising and standing together and facing the flag during the singing. A further modification developed of applauding the professional singer, presumably as a reward for the performance. As
far as I have been able to determine, this occurs only in the
United States, and foreigners often express dismay at the phenomenon. The most recent modification in this development is
heavy applause, even without soloist or group singing, that begins prior to the anthem's conclusion, indeed at times several
bars before the conclusion. This is not limited to sporting events.
It was even evident at the inauguration of George Bush as president of the United States, where the new president himself was
applauding. Group singing of the anthem has virtually disappeared, and with or without a featured singer, it has been replaced by applause.

A related, if less frequently observed phenomenon occurs with
the playing of "Taps." Although Taps is played at military fu-
nerals, it is also played at local Memorial Day ceremonies. The
playing of Taps under such circumstances usually occurs in an
otherwise silent interval, the crowd traditionally bareheaded, the
military personnel at attention.

At several Memorial Day ceremonies in recent years the same
participant applause phenomenon noted for the anthem was
found to occur. People attending the ceremony applauded the
bugler when he had finished playing Taps. Perhaps not so widespread a phenomenon as the applause for "The Star Spangled
Banner," the occurrence is not an isolated one nor one limited
to a particular locale.

In some recent church weddings, after the couple spoke their
vows, the invited guests applauded. Such applause has also become more frequent in churches following sermons and solo
musical performances, although this phenomenon occurs irreg-
ularly.

I have also been in classrooms where the students applauded
the professor at the end of his lecture.

It would seem that in such modifications the attendees cease
to be participants in a ritual and become only spectators at an
event, an *audience*. The ritualistic nature of the activity seems to

have been removed and the event reduced to a performance of an entertainment at which the audience signals its approval by applause. Indeed, this is a conclusion that arose fairly early in these studies, and was tentatively attributed to the destructive effects of the mass media on institutionally supported behaviors. However, the zeal with which the applause is given leads one away from this easy conclusion. Indeed, the fervor with which the participants applaud, particularly in the anthem modification, seems more indicative of the so-called "new nationalism" evidenced in response to the Grenada, Lybian, Panamanian, and Iraqi exploits of recent U.S. administrations.

I consequently turned my attention to studying audiences and observing their activities. However, I found that there have also been changes in audience behaviors that are no less interesting than changes in ritual performances and these deserve a certain amount of attention in order to clarify the preceding.

An audience, in a contemporary sense, does not consist of participants in a communal ritual but of spectators at an entertainment. If we consider some noted historical examples we can discern changes occurring here as well, and these help clarify the nature of the transformation in secular ritual behaviors. Accounts vary, but there seems to be agreement that the premier performance of Igor Stravinsky's *The Rites of Spring* was marked by a riot on the part of an outraged audience, so forceful that Nijinsky and Diaghilev had to flee the opera house and seek refuge in a nearby park. While such a highly involved musical audience may not have existed since, there have been related incidents in more recent decades. For example, in the 1940s the audience at the Metropolitan Opera House in New York did not applaud but booed performances by the baritone Lawrence Tibet, whose voice had been cracking all season but who persisted in giving notoriously bad performances. In the 1950s, when Andre Eglevsky inadvertently dropped Alicia Markova during a performance by Ballet Theater, the audience did not hesitate to boo, signaling its displeasure. Similarly, in the 1960s the audience hissed and booed so loudly when Bob Dylan came on stage with an electric guitar (rather than an acoustical one) at the Newport Folk Festival that he refused to come back on stage for the finale despite coaxing by Pete Seeger, Joan Baez, and others. During the 1970s and 1980s, however, we could find no reports of similar audience behaviors, nor have we witnessed any. To the contrary, audiences at concerts, recitals, and theatrical and dance performances we have attended, or read about, applaud all performances wildly, often giving standing ovations and demanding encores. This is not because the quality of performance has improved dramatically; quite the contrary. Performers are often embarrassed by this new response, for they feel a bad night is rewarded as enthusiastically as a good night, and uncritical use of applause demeans good work. It appears that the audience has grown either tasteless or less sophisticated, or at least, less informed as to the criteria for artistic excellence. Whatever the reason, a change in the behavior of audiences is evident here that seems related to the change noted in behavior at secular rituals. Both phenomena involve applause, and in both categories it is the marked increase and change in the use of applause that is most noticeable.

It would seem at first glance that what distinguishes participants in secular rituals from the audiences at theatrical events is Durkheim's classical distinction between the sacred and the profane; that is, the singing of one's national anthem and such ceremonies as the playing of Taps are sacred in that they refer to "that other realm" of special evaluation, however secular it may be. This gives them their status as ritual. As already noted, participants at a sacred religious ceremony are understood not to comprise a mere audience, but to be partakers of and participants in a ritual celebration seeking communal affinity. Moreover, it is this latter characteristic that clearly distinguishes what might otherwise be considered profane from its secular character. In other words, in order for us to remain true to the Durkheimian concept, not all secular social entities are profane social entities. If this were not so, we could have no secular rituals such as those above. In all these, we found an increase in applause. In the case of the audience, it now appears as payment for any kind of performance, however good or bad, while in the case of mass gatherings it seems to have replaced ritualistic behaviors such as communal singing or the respectful silence following Taps. Nevertheless, it remains a collective response that is here engendered; the audiences and the ritual participants are in both instances united one with another, and display this in their zealous activity. The question is not whether their unity is that of the mob or that of the crusade, but whether they are, in Durkheim's words, in "that state of effervescence... outwardly expressed by exuberant movements which cannot be easily subjected to ends that are too closely defined. They escape, in part, aimlessly, they display themselves for the mere joy of doing so, and take delight in all kinds of games." According to Lukes,[9] "Hence these gestures in the rites which have no purpose but simply respond to the need of the believers to act, to move, to gesticulate, so that one sees them (as Durkheim says) 'jumping, whirling, dancing, crying and singing, though it may not always be possible to give a meaning to this agitation.' " And again, "It plays a role which is by no means negligible. It has its share in that feeling of comfort which the believer draws from the rite performed; for recreation is one of the forms of that moral remaking which is the principal object of the positive rite."[10] It appears that in our cases what has been occurring is a change in the gestures, still expressing "the need of believers to act."

Applause in the case of the anthem and taps has moved from being a gesture hithertofore associated with payment for a performance to a new kind of collective ritualistic behavior; that is to say, the event has not changed from ritual to entertainment, the group from congregation to audience. Rather, whatever group-binding function is still present is now performed by the applause. Thus, the essential demand of the Durkheimian definition of ritual remains satisfied. In applauding the playing of Taps or of "The Star Spangled Banner," the participants are joining each other communally and reaffirming a social bond. This helps us understand their enthusiasm. This amounts to a form of routinization of ritual: instead of being socialized to a vocabulary of differing appropriate responses for disparate ritual occasions, the individuals apply the same ritualized responses to a wide spectrum of ritual events. Differences in meaning among the events become insignificant and finally disappear. The rituals are confined to a redundant format and subsumed within a well-established social form, applause. Although this necessarily marks a change in appearance and performance of the rituals themselves, it is consistent with the leveling phenomenon associated with the routinization process and with the decline in differences that make disparate meanings possible. It does not necessarily eliminate the ritualistic character of the event; it modifies the event in such a way that its uniqueness is minimized or obliterated and the collective response is subsumed under the simplest social form. This may satisfy the needs, or at least some of the needs, previously satisfied by the earlier orthodox form of the ritual.

There are occasions where ad hoc rituals are demanded by the flow of events, often in an attempt to impose meaning on what appears to be a wholly meaningless event. An ad hoc ritual is one that is without a corresponding precedent and hence may lack established protocol. These often occur to commemorate some recent disaster.

According to Durkheim the commemorative ceremony is one example of the ritualistic event.[11] Commemorative rites have the function of "representing or imprinting the past more deeply in the mind." They are ceremonies "whose sole aim is to awaken certain ideas and sentiments, to attach the present to the past or the individual to the collectivity."[12] The examples above are cases where the "aim is . . . to attach the individual to the collectivity." As we have seen, the mechanism for doing this can become routinized. But the second category of Durkheim's commemorative ceremony definition, that of "attaching the present to the past by awakening certain ideas or sentiments" seems more appropriate to specific historical occasions, and it may be that here routinization is less likely to occur than in the circumstances noted above. For example, it sometimes happens that collective traumas occur, such as the Buffalo Creek disaster, which Erikson discusses,[13] or the displacement of an entire Native American population as in the Kinzoa Dam affair of the 1960s, where the Seneca Nation of Indians of upstate New York was forcibly resettled. The question arises, in view of the discussion above, whether the routinization of ritual occurs when ad hoc ceremonies take place commemorating such events as collective traumas. Since these must be planned to suit the occasion, they should be particularly vulnerable to such historical changes as have occurred in the routinization of ritual, such as the substitution of applause for other responsive behavior. On

Table 1

SYRACUSE UNIVERSITY
Memorial Service
Twelve O'Clock Noon
Wednesday, the Eighteenth of January
Nineteen Hundred and Eighty-Nine
The Carrier Dome
PROGRAM

Organ Prelude		Katherine F.Pardee
"Lament for the Children" (traditional)	Arr. by J. Avery Head	
	Syracuse Scottish Pipe Band	
Words of Welcome and Invocation	Rev. Dr.Richard L. Phillips,	
	Dean of Hendricks Chapel	
"Cast Thy Burden Upon the Lord"(from Elijah) Felix Mendelssohn		
"Lacrymosa" (from Requiem)		W.A. Mozart
	Syracuse University Combined Choruses	
	The Syracuse Symphony Orchestra	
	Kazuyoshi Akimayama, Conductor	
In Tribute	The Honorable Thomas G. Young	
	Mayor of the City of Syracuse	
In Tribute	The Honorable Alfonse M. D'Amato	
	Senator of the United States	
In Tribute	The Honorable Daniel P. Moynihan	
	Senator of the United States	
In Tribute	The Honorable Mario M. Cuomo	
	Governor of the State of New York	
"Nimrod"	(from Enigma variations)	Edward Elgar
	The Syracuse Symphony Orchestra	
	Kazuyoshi Akiyama, Conductor	
In Tribute	The Reverend Monsignor Charles Borgognoni	
In Tribute	Rabbi Milton H. Elefant	
In Tribute	The Reverend Dr. Paul J. Kowalewski	
"Salvation is Created"		Paul Tschesnokoff
	Syracuse University Combined Choruses	
	G. Burton Harbison, Conductor	
In Tribute	John M. Mandyck	President of the Student
		Government Association
In Tribute	Douglas A. Unger	Professor of English
In Tribute	Melvin A. Eggers	Chancellor
Benediction		
Organ Postlude		Dr. Katherine F. Pardee

the other hand, it may be that the very nature of trauma requires more traditional procedures to evoke an appropriate response.

With these considerations in mind, it is useful to consider one example of such an ad hoc ritual: the memorial service that took place on January 18, 1989 in the Carrier Dome on the campus of Syracuse University. Mourners met to commemorate the thirty Syracuse students killed the previous month on Pan American Flight 103 as they attempted to return home from their studies in London.

Table 1 reproduces the order of the service, attended by parents of the deceased students, townspeople, faculty, students, and staff. The institutionalized, collective nature of the commemorative event is evident throughout the table. Representatives of church and state and the academy conducted the service. The political institution was represented by the mayor of the city, the governor of the state, and both United States senators. There is another dimension of interest: one U.S. senator (D'Amato) is an alumnus of this university, the other (Moynihan) has served on its Social Science faculty and the governor is himself a former professor, having taught at St. John's University in New York. So the educational institution was strongly symbolized. They were joined by the Protestant, Catholic, and Jewish chaplains, and by the dean of the interdenominational campus chapel, all symbolizing the religious institution. The president of the student association and a professor from the London program also spoke, and the chancellor of the university (not a clergyman) delivered the benediction. The service began with the dean of the chapel signaling the people to rise; everyone did so, in complete silence, as the bagpipe band, out of sight in some corridor, played the *Lament for the Children*.

The entire program shown in Table 1 was conducted in complete silence on the part of those who attended. The Carrier Dome, particularly in the basketball season (when this event took place) can be an outrageously noisy place. Many of the students and faculty present at the memorial service are regular subscribers to the sports programs, and those we interviewed were struck by the absolute silence of the place during this event. In addition, the fourteen fraternities and sororities at this university were all represented: the young men entering together and sitting in groups in their "suits and ties," the young women in "dresses and heels," a very unusual sight on a contemporary American campus in the middle of a day of classes. Since by this time I had become aware of the routinization of ritual events, and particularly of the new role played by applause, I expected at least some of the attendees to applaud, if not after the bagpipes, at least after the orchestra or the singing of the chorus. However, not a single person among the 15,000 applauded at any time, and when the program had concluded, they quietly departed.

It may be that the ad hoc and funereal nature of the event

precluded such behavior as applause. But as we have seen, a funereal situation did not prevent applause from occurring for the Memorial Day buglers. The fact that no one knew "how one was supposed to act" at such an occasion, the lack of precedent may have been more persuasive since nothing of this sort had taken place on campus before. This might have encouraged planners and participants to fall back upon traditional expectations regarding personal demeanor at ritual events. The choice of speakers, the order of service, as well as the student response of suit-tie, dress-heels, for example, may indicate this. On the other hand, orchestras and choruses are usually applauded, (sometimes in simple error, as at the closing of a movement of a symphony when part of the audience does not realize that only a movement has been played) and no applause took place for them here. Or, and I find this more persuasive, it may be that the collective trauma experienced by the community evoked a solemnity at the ceremony that precluded certain forms of visible "agitation" such as described by Durkheim, but "It (still) played a role which is by no means negligible. It has its share in that feeling of comfort which the believer draws from the rite performed." In this case, traditional activities incorporated into the ad hoc event seem to have precluded the newer, routinized response of applause. That the comfort Durkheim mentions did indeed occur is quite clear. From the standpoint of sociological discourse, it is interesting that all the major social institutions were symbolically represented at the service, together with the community at large representing civil society merging with the academic community to evoke whatever fragments of meaning were possible. It would seem that this signals the kind of "communal-centric" ceremony not unlike that confronting the polis present at an ancient Greek tragedy. In addition, it points to the deep need for symbolic representation of grief at the level of the community, for which no other social mechanism is available but funerary ritual, in whatever form it is given. Death is by its very nature meaningless, and the death of these young college students under such conditions only emphasized its meaninglessness. The ad hoc nature of the event and the behavior of its participants is in marked contrast with the routinized celebration of the Memorial Day event with its increasingly routinized responses. Although both are funerary in nature, applause appears to have become a routinized response to a wide variety of collective gatherings routinely celebrated, such as Memorial Day, but may still be an inappropriate response for specific ad hoc memorial occasions.

Processes of routinization and demystification may occur in secular as well as in sacred contexts, minimizing the differences in meanings between these contexts. In spite of increasing attempts to secularize all social activity, including holidays, there appears to be a continuing need for the comfort, healing, and commemorative effects rituals perform, particularly in the face of otherwise meaningless tragedy. Unknowingly confronting the death of meaning, individuals may find themselves demanding some kind of ritualistic ceremony to reassure them that even in the face of ultimate oblivion there is solace and comfort to be found. They demand meaning in the face of the meaningless. This may also help us understand why certain religious holidays have proven resistant to government and commercial manipulation. But this may also lead to the redundant application of a particular secular activity to a wide range of ritual events, as the introduction of applause where other responses more imbued with meaning had previously been employed.

NOTES

1. Max Weber, *The Sociology of Religion* (Boston: Beacon Press, 1963), 86.

2. George V. Zito. (1983). "Toward a Sociology of Heresy." *Sociological Analysis* 44(2), 123–130.

3. David Martin, *A General Theory of Secularization* (New York: Harper and Row), 1979.

4. See George V. Zito, *Systems of Discourse: Structures and Semiotics in the Social Sciences* (Westport, Conn.: Greenwood Press), 1984; see also Malcolm Bull. 1989. "Seventh Day Adventists: Heretics of American Civil Religion." *Sociological Analysis* 50 2, 177–187.

5. Robert Bellah, *The Broken Covenant* (New York: Seabury), 1975.

6. See Mircea Eliade, *The Sacred and the Profane* (New York: Harcourt Brace and Jovanovich), 1959.

7. Emile Durkheim, *The Elementary Forms of the Religious Life* (New York: Free Press), 1969; Steven Lukes, *Emile Durkheim, His Life and Work*

(Middlesex: Penguin Books), 1973; Ernest Wallwork, *Durkheim: Morality and Milieu* (Cambridge, Mass.: Harvard University Press), 1972.

8. Mircea Eliade, 1959, 184ff.

9. Lukes, 1973, 469ff.

10. Durkheim, 1969, 379–383; Lukes, 1973, 471.

11. Durkheim, 1969.

12. Durkheim, 376–378.

13. Kai T. Erikson, *Everything in its Path* (New York: Simon and Schuster), 1976.

Chapter 4

Defusing Discourse

Other destructive practices have become prevalent in addition to the routinization and equalization already discussed. The contribution of these practices to the death of meaning is more subtle. But if meanings lie primarily in the relations among things, in their differences, then any behavior that minimizes or eliminates differences constitutes an attack upon meanings. Similarly, any behavior that attempts to immediately destroy or replace one meaning with another already at hand is an attack upon the very nature of meanings, since it renders irrelevant that which is preferred *only because it is that which is preferred.* This is not merely a change in meaning that is being targeted here. Meanings have histories and meanings change. But when an intended meaning is dismissed *only because it is intended,* then the very nature of meaning is being dismissed for the gratification of the power demands of the person or group furnishing such a dismissal.

This happens frequently in conversation, where the denotative power of intended meaning is defused by respondents in their replies to assertions made by their companions. It occurs, too, at a more complex level, where institutionalized structures, such as publishing, education and the media, play their parts in constructing the social reality of the particular time and place.

In interactions between individuals, defusing occurs when conversation is redirected from its intended meaning in order to serve the ego and power demands of a participant seeking to impose his or her will upon the social interaction and hence dominate definitions of social situations. The related processes, occurring at the institutional level of discourse suggests that these are not simply similar but conceptually identical, and reflect the willful demands of participants.

We can define *discourse* as any activity ordering its concerns through language.[1] This definition includes those made by Foucault[2] for the institutionalized level as well as the interactional, conversational activity analyzed by Sacks,[3] and Scott and Lyman.[4] Foucault and his French associates were interested in the constraints imposed upon discourse generally, but paid particular attention to those occurring in the academy, in publishing, in the mental hospital, in prisons and in sexuality: in other words, in discourse in the larger, macroscopic level. The work on verbal conversations among and between individuals carried on by Harvey Sacks and other Americans derives from the work of Harold Garfinkle[5] and considers how ordinary people maintain social and verbal interaction in the face of imperfect, imprecise, or unknowable information. It asks the question, What are the mutual but unspoken agreements (tacit understandings) that perpetuate the construction of social realities? Thus, unlike the efforts of Foucault and his associates, this American enterprise was limited primarily to the personal interactional (or microsocial) level.

Despite their differences in focus, both the American and the French enterprises considered discourses, in the sense of the definition offered above. Both sought to clarify the wholly social nature of our understanding and therefore of the meanings we associate with happenings in the "real" world about us. Both challenge taken-for-granted assumptions regarding the nature of apparent "truths" and the ability of the individual to make sense out of an apparently haphazard, unfriendly life world.

At the level of verbal interaction among individuals something occurs, similar to the furnishing of an account, or a disclaimer, and related to what used to be termed "one up-manship" but distinct from it. This is the defusing or emasculation of the content of conversation to render it central to the ego demands of the responding individual.

The political or power dimension present in interpersonal interactional events has been recognized by various schools of sociology, by feminists and others.[6] It is not generally considered that the macrosocial case, to be considered later, also contains such a distortion of intended meaning in an effort to center power on the deflecting group at the expense of others. The pattern in the microsocial, interactional case is a familiar one, and we have all had occasion to witness it and employ it; nevertheless, it is worth providing some observed examples of it here. Examples of the macrosocial case will be presented later in this chapter.

The following examples are drawn from real life situations studied by the author and are typical manifestations of the defusing phenomenon.

Individual A: "It took us ten miles, down a pitted dirt road to the dock where we could put in our canoe. We loaded on five gallons of water, our tent, sleeping bags and supplies and had to paddle into the face of a strong wind for another four miles or so. But when we made camp it all seemed worth it! Miles of sandy beaches with no one around. Primitive camping at its best. It was worth it!"

Individual B: "Yes, I know. I once had to drive ten miles down a dirt road in Vermont to get to a lake. What lake was that? I've forgotten."

In this simple example, we see defusing by B. It is clear that what excites A and what he wishes to communicate to B is his "wonderful experience of primitive canoe camping." But B deflects the direction of A's meaning by misreading, or perhaps pretending to misread, A's meaning and substitutes the least desirable element of the account, the drive down a pitted dirt road, making it the principal focus of the communication.

Another example:

Individual A: "She loves her work out West! She does all kinds of environmental work planting grasses to restore strip-mined areas, operating bulldozers, building wild bird rookeries. She even flies with a pilot in a small plane every week to estimate the size of animal herds by sampling techniques, or the number of hawks in a given area."

Individual B: "I had to do some sampling in college: fruit flies I think it was. And the Michaelson oil drop experiment where you try to figure the mass of an electron. I don't like estimating populations; that's boring stuff."

This example is more blatantly extreme, but contains the same element of defusing. In both examples the discussion is deflected by the respondent B to his or her own experience, in effect dismissing the thrust of A's discussion to himself as subject and placing the emphasis elsewhere than A intended. In the second example, B moves the focus from the wide variety of outdoor activities and the excitement such variety involves to a stress on emphasizing the size of a population from a sample. These are not examples of simple "one-up manship" where the respondent attempts to outdo the original speaker by a more grandiose accounting. Here the speaker has his or her meaning distorted and trivialized by the respondent. Nor are these accounts of the Scott-Lyman variety, where respondents seek to explain away untoward activity in terms they believe their listener will accept, or of disclaimers seeking to divorce the speaker from responsibility for some action. What is especially interesting is that should A attempt to correct B, the correction would likely be similarly defused by B, leaving A frustrated in the attempt to communicate intended meaning. A growing impatience on the part of A sometimes occurs, and should the process continue, A may break off the interaction. Indeed, in some cases I have witnessed, A may shun B in the future and markedly limit or preclude possible interactions with B.

One further example should be sufficient to make the point being sought.

Individual A: "It was so different from the street during the day! We turned on to Lexington Avenue from Twenty-First Street and ran smack into a scene out of a grade B movie! Talk about stereotypes! These poor teen age girls, overflowing their too tight clothes and smeared with cheap makeup just stared impassively at the men going by, their pimps sitting in jazzed-up cars at the curb. It was tragic and trite at the same time, you know? that run down, big city atmosphere. The police cars slowly drove by, pointedly ignoring everything. The people rushing by, the noise, the smells."

Individual B: "Oh, yeah. I've seen prostitutes when we lived in Texas. There was a little 'boys' town' across the border, with Mexican girls."

Here respondent B changes the stress from big-city atmosphere to merely "seeing prostitutes." In all these cases a narrative is furnished and the respondent, who has not shared in the experience recounted, attempts to compensate for the exclusion by shifting the emphasis to some nonsalient aspect of the account which is either commonplace or of marginal significance and pretends that this is the focus of the speaker's story, in effect displacing the narrator in favor of himself or herself.

The above are examples of dyadic interactions. Examples may also be drawn from larger groups. Many of us have been at department or committee meetings (for example) where a policy decision must be made and the topic is raised or read as a prepared statement. Participants at such meetings who are staff members feel obliged to speak. In the case of a college faculty meeting, Professor A responds first, speaking not directly to the matter at hand but intentionally or otherwise defusing it into a channel more familiar to himself. Thus, he may begin by invoking "reductionism" and "logical fallacies" which he claims obscure the real issues that need considering. Professor B then feels compelled to speak at least as long as Professor A, and takes up the deflected discourse into channels more central to himself, rather than to Professor A, as for example "the danger of employing technological metaphors in a consideration of this kind." The process continues around the room, with each speaker deflecting the discourse an additional increment away from its earlier subject. If, as sometimes happens, the matter comes up for a vote, the group may vote on the motion without having really discussed it at all. If not, the meeting ends in disorder. I have chosen this example because it is familiar to many of us, in one context or another, whether a town council or Board of Education meeting, a PTA or volunteer organization session, or the "deliberation" of a more august body. Sometimes after such a meeting the participants may claim that a great deal was accomplished although, when pressed, they are not able to verbalize its precise nature; later they may experience a sense of having been somehow duped, or misled. It is clear that here, too, the successive acts of defusing may work against long-term sociating processes and preclude further group interaction. Group members may experience varying degrees of disorientation—cognitive dissonance—and feel progressively isolated from one another.

At the macrosocial level of discourse, individuals tend to be less significant and a collectivity performs the activity that is essentially the same as microsocial defusing. Much work has already been done in analyzing the discourse of sexuality by Foucault,[7] but little attention has been given to recent alterations in the American component of this discourse.

In English, "sexual intercourse," as defined by the *Oxford English Dictionary*, denotes coital activity whereas "sex" denotes a condition of being, anatomical differences between males and females. The recent substitution of the phrase "having sex" for the former phrase deflects the emphasis of its meaning from wholly coital activity to any activity involving sexuality. The "having" defuses the activity to a recreational one, on the level of "having a coke," or "having a beer," or simply "having fun." It then follows that where the level is one of "having," one has a choice, an option or preference. The matter of homosexuality, for example, accordingly becomes just one other option, one's "sexual preference," rather than negatively sanctioned behavior. Whatever traditional feelings had been associated with it are consequently defused, as Victorian notions of guilt were defused by the recreational transformation of "having sex."

Similarly, if "sex" is used to denote the *activity* rather than an *anatomical condition,* then maleness and femaleness may be designated in ways that are not anatomically specific but socially generated. "Gender," hitherto the property of nouns, may be used to denote these conditions, effectively reducing sexual differences to a "way of speaking" rather than to a "way of being": anatomy becomes defined by *words* rather than *things.* Something similar occurred with respect to "androgyny," a word signifying the hermaphroditic condition of having sexual organs (or the parts thereof) of both sexes. Again, the *Oxford English Dictionary* is the reference here. Having wholly social or behavioral characteristics of both sexes is signified in English by the word "epicene." The original Epicene, however, is a character in a comedy by Ben Jonson: Shakespeare's contemporary satirized the sexually liberated women of seventeenth-century England.[8] The word is accordingly avoided in current sexist discourse. In substituting "androgyny" for "epicene" something similar occurs: in the first case a word signifying anatomical differences (sex) has been replaced by one signifying a grammatical difference (gender), and in the second case a word signifying an anatomical difference (androgyny) has been substituted for one signifying behavioral differences (epicene). Meaning here becomes obscured and tenuous. Groups fostering their own redefinitions of social situations confound the possibility of meanings by being trapped in a kind of dialectical prison; the ideological assertions of their rhetorics contain immanent contradictions which can lead them in either direction in their efforts to impose their wills through alternative definitions of social realities. As a result, they are seldom logically consistent in the internal structuring of their arguments. Sometimes such rhetorical efforts are abandoned when attempts to impose redefinition fails. For a short time, "elderly maiden" was attempted to signify the "adult bachelor girl," but it conjured up for many the earlier rejected "old maid" and had to be abandoned. Similarly, attempts to substitute other designations for "common-law husband (or wife)" have proven difficult; anything from "roommate" through "live-in lover" to "significant other" is attempted, but no clear-cut designation has emerged to escape the perceived opprobrium of the earlier term.

I have chosen these examples because of their currency, rather than their participation in particular ideologies, although some of these defuses seem to have been introduced by the "women's movement." The initial transmutation to "having sex," however, appears to have arisen in popular culture as a consequence of the intrusion into its parlance of expressions of "having," for example: "What'll you have?" or "She's having a ball" or "I've been had," possibly compensating for a limitation in the increasingly widespread use of adolescent vocabularies. Indeed, the various forms of "to have" seem as frequent as "like" or "yuh know?" and similar expressions of adolescent cultures. Thus, an original deflection may arise from traditional etymological sources and affect cognitive and lexical processes in directions that lend themselves to ideological postures of protesting or otherwise vocal social groups or political parties. These latter are examples of defusings in discourse that are beyond the dyadic or small group interactional levels; they involve newspapers and magazines, published texts, organizations and related structures that institutionalize (or seek to institutionalize) particular ways of defining the world and by doing so enhance the power positions of specific groups. These may then become imbedded in their rhetoric and thence be taken for granted as truths or truisms requiring no additional justification.

Sometimes a group, pursuing its power impulses, exacts changes in the use of a word or words that are consequences of its members' ignorance of language and meanings. The word "chair*man*," for example, is not male specific; the word root is from the Latin *manus*, or hand, signifying one who "holds" the chair, or operates it, as in *manage*. "Chairperson," on the other hand, is meaningless, unless it signifies a masked (persona) piece of furniture.

Both the interactional and the institutional examples discussed above contain the identical patterning I have been referring to as defusing. They decenter the focus of discourse from the speaker (in the one case) or the culture (in the other case) and turn it to the advantage of the respondent or ideological political group seeking to dominate others. Thus, the ego concern of the defuser attempts to impose itself upon the discussion. All discourse, after all, whether microsocial or macrosocial, involves an attempt at control, an effort to dominate definitions of situations.[9] In the microsocial examples the respondent left out of the experience performs the deflection in order to place himself or herself at the center, thus asserting that Nietzschean will to power that has so influenced later "postmodern" writers. In doing so, however, the individual not only constrains the direction of interaction but may alienate the other and cause the interaction to abort, or severely limit the possibility that interaction with this person will again occur in the future.

In the anxiety to place his or her own self at the center, the individual may be truly seeking to institute or maintain an interaction with the other (may indeed be thirsting for interaction in a society where increasing fragmentation progressively isolates one from others). But this condition either does not obtain or at most occurs only momentarily. In the macrosocial examples, collective efforts are made to satisfy the power demands of larger segments of a population by attempting to institutionalize ways of discussing social phenomena in the press, in publishing generally and in educational and political arenas. But such efforts constrain the discourse by defusing it and directing it into channels that make the collectivity preferring it central to the discourse, where they had hitherto been only marginal or at best, estranged. Here too the risk exists of exacerbating the estrangement rather than mitigating it, if the defusing reduces interactional phenomena among groups rather than enhancing it. Defusing at both levels appears at such times to run counter to the apparent intention of the defusing individual or group. In striving to place themselves at the center of the social situation and dominate the direction of discourse for their own personal or political ends, they may inadvertently be forced further to the periphery by the very defusing they introduce to mitigate the estrangement. Here the dialectical or contradictory possibility manifests itself.

The discussion above suggests that we have now come full circle, and that American sociologists immersed in ethnomethodology and symbolic interactionism with a history quite discreet from their European colleagues are nevertheless exploring the same phenomenon as their French colleagues, the only social phenomenon open to their varieties of analysis, language itself. Language is a kind of social system, the only concern of which is meanings.[10] Meanings are attributed by participants, and participants are probably as often wrong as right in attempting to decode meanings, whether this takes place in personal interactions between two or more people or at the broader, institutional level.

Defusing attacks meaning by substituting, for the intended meaning of the originating speaker or agency, some other meaning that places the respondent or protester at the center and makes the respondent's concern a new "intended" meaning, stripping the original of its communicative force and origin. Certain followers of the French thinker Jacques Derrida[11] so "deconstruct" texts, substituting their own meanings for the meanings of the author, and claim that this is a legitimate procedure. But this kind of literary indulgence is not our concern unless it leads to defusing at the interactional or collective levels; highly subjectivist indulgences have always abounded for those who choose to make use of them.

The defusing phenomenon does not create changes in meanings; the substituted meaning already existed as a possibility and was simply injected by the respondent, not for the purpose of clarification, but because of his or her ego demands and the corresponding will to power, the emotional need of the respondent to place its own self at the center. The loss of the speaker's intended meaning by this substitution renders the effort of the speaker meaningless. Thus, as meanings decline individuals are thrown back on themselves in a world where all activity begins to appear pointless. The assertions of self in the act of defusing is a desperate cry for help, an appeal against being omitted, left out, superseded by changes over which one experiences only one's own powerlessness, one's own estrangement.

NOTES

1. This definition and its implications have been explored more fully in Zito, 1983, and has been expanded upon by Bull, 1989, and others.

2. Michel Foucault, 1972.

3. Harvey Sacks, "An Initial Investigation of the Usability of Conversational Data," in D. Sudnow (ed.), *Studies in Interaction* (New York: Free Press), 1972.

4. Marvin B. Scott and Stanford Lyman, 1968, 46–62.

5. Harold Garfinkle, 1967.

6. Clark, 1957, 317n.

7. Michel Foucault, *The History of Sexuality, Vol. I* (New York: Vintage), 1980; *The Use of Pleasure, Vol. 2, The History of Sexuality* (New York: Vintage), 1986; *Care of the Self, Vol. 3, The History of Sexuality* (New York: Pantheon), 1986.

8. The "Ladies Collegiate" of the play *Epicene* who practice birth control, refer to each other by their last names, etc., a group that in real life included Penelope Rich, the sister of Essex, as well as the prototype of Spenser's Stella.

9. See, in this connection, Harvey L. Molotch and Deidre Boden. 1985. "Talking Social Structure: Discourse, Domination and the Watergate Hearings." *American Sociological Review* 50, 273–287. 1985.

10. It is an "autopoietic system" of the kind discussed by Luhmann in contemporary German sociology, a system that produced more of its own kinds of systems, systems of meanings producing meanings. See Niklas Luhmann, *Love as Passion* (Cambridge, Mass.: Harvard University Press), 1986.

11. See Derrida, 1976.

Chapter 5

The Raping of Rape

At this point it is appropriate to look at attempts to alter meanings in such a way as to emphasize their cathectical and emotive property rather than whatever denotative or instrumental content they contain. This operation, while apart from the operation designated as defusing, places an additional burden of confusion on the individual who attempts to decode intended meanings, to search for the meaning of a meaning: that is, to search for what the meaning designates in an instrumental sense. I have chosen a highly emotionally charged social phenomenon as the initial step in defining this operation: the problem of rape. Here it is useful to rephrase the question posed by Foucault in his *History of Sexuality* series: Why is it that while insisting that we suffer sexual repression, a discourse on rape has developed that insists that rape, an essentially male activity, is not a sexual activity but a violent activity, and simultaneously maintains that it should not be covered by the ordinary laws prohibiting and punishing violent assault?

Rape is "the act of *taking* anything by force; violent seizure (of goods)," according to the first definition in the *Oxford English Dictionary* (OED), the standard reference to the language. What characterizes rape is violence, force, seizure "of goods" of whatever kind. George Bush's war in the Persian Gulf was therefore a rape of Iraq. The unremitting ferocity unleashed against the inhabitants of Baghdad in the face of little resistance is characteristic of such rapes, taking from them their personal freedom at the threat of death. George Bush and the Americans were not alone in committing this rape; they had French, British, and Saudi Arabian confederates.

According to the historical definition, the meaning of *rape* is to take *anything* by force. This is how Chaucer understood the meaning of the English word in 1386. Much earlier, the "rape of the Sabine women" by the emerging Roman tribesmen, celebrated in art and legend, involved the Romans capturing the women and carrying them off, in effect kidnapping them. Similarly, Paris' "rape of Helen" involved his stealing her away from Menelaus and carrying her off to Troy. Neither Helen nor the Sabine women were penetrated against their wills, and neither seems to have objected to being carried off (indeed, it was Menelaus who complained loudly to his brother Agamemnon to call up the Aachaens and send an expedition to recapture the stolen woman and return her to her husband). In 1712 Alexander Pope wrote "Rape of the Lock," a poem celebrating an actual event in which Lord Petre spontaneously snipped off a lock of hair from the head of Arabella Fermer and carried it off in spite of her objections and the outrage of her family.

Definitions are attempts at specifying instrumental meanings: the meanings of words. Rape is a word with several possible meanings. The association of rape with women is the second usage listed by the OED. It is similar to the first, except that "anything" is replaced by "a person, esp. a woman": "The act of carrying away a person, esp. a woman, by force." The rape of Helen of Troy and of the Sabine women fits this definition. They were carried off by their abductors. Thus, the first definition is characterized by its inclusion of violence and seizure; the second by a form of forceful kidnapping of a person. The third usage listed is "violation or ravishing of a woman," and the OED quotes a publication by Caxton in 1481, which includes, "He forced my wife—this is murder, rape and treason." Again, this definition derives not from the "carrying away" element of the second definition but the use of force in both definitions, and such force is here equated with murder and treason in its viciousness.

Thus, it is quite clear that rape is not a sexual crime but a crime of violence. The victim of a rape may be a nation (Iraq), a people (Sabines, Jews, Croats, Poles, Gypsies), an individual (Helen), or any object or goods forcibly taken from another (a lock of hair). Shakespeare's long poem of 1594, "The Rape of Lucrece," involved the rape of a Roman woman. Lucretia had been awarded a prize for her chastity, and Sextus Tarquinus here breaks into her bedchamber and "ravishes" her, corresponding to the action of the third definition above. Thus, "by force" he "carries away" her "chastity." Here the association of the word is with the act of deprivation: he "carries away" something of hers, takes it by force and violence. Similarly, in Shakespeare's early play, *Titus Andronicus,* the two depraved brothers "ravish" Lavinia, carrying away not only her virginity but her tongue and hands lest she be able to identify them. Hence, although rape is not in itself a sexual phenomenon, it may involve sexually oriented activities in some of its many forms. Indeed, the sexual association was sometimes used by Shakespeare in the form of analogies, as in King John (II,i): "Thou hast done a rape . . . upon the maiden virtue of the crown." Here again, however, the association is a mixed one: "maiden virtue" recalls the first two definitions: maidenhood is here virginity, and this has been carried away by force. The third definition is hardly involved.

Nevertheless it is clear that one form of violent seizure involves the taking of something sexual. Male prisoners when forced to engage in homosexual activities are considered victims of rape. Homosexual males have also been raped by other homosexual or bisexual males. Reports of such incidents always involve the use of violent force against resisting victims. But it is also clear that the sexual embodiment of rape is only one particular embodiment of the concept of rape, and only one application of the word itself. According to the OED, rape in 1390 was a kind of turnip; earlier, in the *Domesday Book,* it was a unit of measure similar to a chain or mile; by 1502 it was a rough file (later changed to 'rasp'?) and as canary fanciers know, it is still a variety of aromatic bird seed.

At times of more relaxed tensions between the sexes, Ogden Nash could quip, "Seduction is for sissies/But a He-man wants his rape." This sexual association of the word has grown in intensity and is particularly salient at a time when hostility between the sexes is unusually strong, as at the present. Radical feminists have seized upon the word in their war against everything male or masculine. Rape has become the battle cry on campuses and Womens Studies programs across the United States, and the press and other media are quick to seize upon any incident of a sexual nature, however incidental, to further the public's craving for the salacious and sensational.[1]

Although most feminists agree that "rape is not a sexual crime, it is a crime of violence," they have sought to shift the meaning away from the element of violence to the element of "consent," insisting that "when a woman says 'no' she means no," and therefore any vaginal penetration of a female by a male thereafter constitutes rape. They have even fought to have laws changed in several states reflecting this change in meaning. This has subsequently led to the invention of a category feminists label *date rape*. In this usage any penetration of a female who says "no" constitutes rape, whether it involves force or violence or not. Aside from the implicit logical contradiction here—the definition's minimizing of the element of violence and maximizing the element of consent, while simultaneously insisting that this is a crime of violence and not a sexual crime—the semiotic problem is significant. Radical feminists have insisted for years that when a woman says "yes" to a man she does not necessarily mean "yes": she has been socialized to say yes to men even when she means no. But if a man is not to believe a woman when she says yes, it is not clear why he should believe her when she says no. The implication is that women are socialized as young girls to say yes to men for everything but to say no to sex, an empirically sound observation about the socialization of many girls in American society that is reflected in the popular literature. The corollary of this from the male perspective is to question whether a woman means no when she says yes (Is she just placating me because I'm a man?) and yes when she says no (Is she just playing hard to get or feigning a traditional virtue she clearly does not possess?). American males have traditionally been expected to be aggressive in all matters, including sexual ones (even when they don't wish to be) and females have traditionally been expected to be passive in all matters including sexual ones (even when they don't wish to be). A sexually aggressive female is apt to scare off a less than aggressive male and confound an aggressive one.

Human sexual activity is a social activity; it is a form (or forms) of interaction. Males and females tend to play out their sexual roles as they do other social roles, as consequences of their socialization. Males in American society are socialized to be sexually aggressive but are not socialized to commit rapes; females are socialized to pretend virtuous resistance to sexual encounters but to fight off rapists. However, the degrees of freedom within the norms of socialization are few and far between, particularly where interactions between unlike partners are concerned and where socialization has become increasingly peer group derived, rather than family, church, and adult community derived, and where these peer groups are largely same-sex groups. The language of one peer group may not be the language of another: although the words may sound and spell the same, the intended meanings may be completely different.

The differences in the meanings of words as a function of sex or gender has been explored by Deborah Tannen in her book *You Just Don't Understand: Women and Men in Conversation.*[2] Her research shows clearly that for American women, from girlhood on, talk is associated with intimacy in a way it is not for men and boys. Men and boys take charge more aggressively than girls and women, and this is reflected in their speech and actions. Each group misunderstands the other, and each seeks to make the other conform to their definitions of things. What a man is apt to understand by no in a sexual (or any intimate) situation and what a woman claims she means by no (in a sexual or any intimate situation) usually do not coincide. This is what led to the invention of so-called "date rape," where a woman reports that she said no but he went ahead and penetrated her anyway. The invention of date rape has not been covered by Tannen; it has, however, been discussed by feminist Ellen Goodman, a widely syndicated newspaper columnist of Boston. In her article, "Both Often Believe They're Right in Date Rape," Goodman concludes that "we still live in a culture in which he says date and she says rape. And each fervently calls the other a liar."[3] Both are right because they understand the word(s) differently. Radical feminists, however, are less apt than Goodman to make such a concession. This was particularly evident in the case of vocalist Holly Dunn, a country music singer whose record "Maybe I Mean Yes," was banned from radio in Los Angeles when the radical feminist Leah Aldridge of the Los Angeles Commission of Assaults Against Women complained about the lines, "Nothin's worth having if it ain't a little hard to get . . . When I say no I mean maybe. Or maybe I mean yes." Aldrich complained that the song "encouraged date rape." Dunn was shocked by this alien ideological interpretation of her lyrics and by the subsequent censorship imposed by the record company. She said her song was intended as "a lighthearted look at one couple's attempt at dating, handled in an innocent, non-sexual, flirtatious way."[4] Dunn's understanding is that of American men and women generally, but radical feminists have sometimes influenced the courts in the way typified by censors such as Aldrich. In most states the person accused of rape cannot be convicted on the basis of words: there must be physical evidence of violence, something that can be seen and measured and evaluated objectively. Radical-feminist pressure has been successful, in some states, such as New York, in removing the requirement of objective evidence and relying wholly upon the word of the female accuser. Such a procedure adds another weapon to the radical feminist arsenal against men.

The popular understanding of the situation has been voiced recently by Ann Landers, one of the most widely syndicated columnists in the country. In an article entitled, "Physical Signs Should Tell Woman When To Yell 'Stop,' "[5] Landers concludes, "The female who agrees to hours of petting but does not want to complete the sex act is asking for trouble and she probably will get it. The notion that a woman has the right to change her mind after two hours of passionate stimulation may be legally sound but it flies in the face of the most basic facts of procreation and biological human drives." Although this position is apt to arouse charges of "blaming the victim," it is clear that it represents a widely accepted popular view. In addition, victims very often may indeed be rightly subjected to blame.

Any student of victimization knows that some categories of persons are victimized more than others, and that victimization is often a form of social interaction involving both parties. Thus, the Law Enforcement Assistance Administration studies of victimization in target cities[6] were able to generate profiles of those persons most likely to be victimized, the time of day and the places victimization was most likely to occur. Victims of any kind of assault may unwittingly or even knowingly participate in these kinds of interactions. The prominent sociologist Stanford Lyman spent many years teaching on the West Coast, and was offered a position on a respected graduate faculty in New York City. He accepted the position. His West Coast colleagues warned him that if he lived in New York City he would likely get mugged, but he dismissed their concern as regional bias. On his very first day in New York City, however, he decided to visit Times Square, and was rubbernecking the sights when he was indeed mugged. He decided his West Coast colleagues had been correct, but when he nonchalantly mentioned the incident the next day to his New York colleagues, they were shocked. Although they had lived in the city for many years, none of them had ever been mugged there. Upon questioning him, the city dwellers decided that Lyman had, by unwittingly acting like a tourist, made himself the target of a mugger. He agreed, and often related the story to his students and colleagues. It is important to note that Lyman "made himself" a victim here, and no one blamed him for the victimization: the blame remains on the mugger for the incident itself. But city dwellers all over the world learn certain coping techniques to avoid victimization, and Lyman if he had learned them, forgot to practice them on his first day in New York. Thus, his socialization respecting conduct in big cities was either lacking a critical element or he forgot himself for a moment and made himself a target.

One more relevant "victim" was Carolyn Ossen, a college freshman who accompanied a black basketball recruit to his hotel room in an upstate city, where she encouraged him to undress her and perform oral sex upon her, and then accused him of "date rape" when he penetrated her. He was arrested, lost his attempt at a scholarship, was banned at several colleges, and his name was announced in many newspapers, effectively killing a possible sports career. Her name was not at first revealed by the press, following a policy that precludes publishing names of such sexual "victims." The athlete was subsequently exonerated when the defense produced a videotape of Ossen with her girlfriends, made prior to the incident, in which she boasts of repeatedly seeking out black athletes for sex, encouraging them to have oral sex on her and then feigning sleeping or employing some other ruse as a way out of "going all the way," and leaving them frustrated. This kind of vicious exploitation of the male caused the judge to rule the basketball player the "victim" in this case and he was exonerated of all but the most trivial charges. His possible career, however, has gone down the drain. The local press finally relented and published Ossen's name. Later, she sought to shift the blame to the young women who had introduced her to the player and who had furnished him with a condom on her behalf. After the revelation of the videotape and the exoneration of the player by the judge, Ossen discovered that her classmates found her unacceptable. She quit the school, bitterly denouncing the judge, the player, her classmates, and her women friends. Outraged radical feminists then sought to heap blame upon the judge, who had acted upon the recommendation of a female prosecutor.

The invention of date rape and the usual classification of the woman as a "victim" has caused an upheaval in legal circles with respect to the concealing of the so-called "victim's" name. If, as generally agreed, rape is a crime of violence and not a sex crime, then it should be treated by the press as any other violent crime is treated by the press, and the names of the offended parties published. Newspapers seldom hesitate to publish the names of victims of violence. By deciding a priori that the woman who claims to have been raped is a "victim" and the accused man is a "perpetrator" of a violent criminal act prior to trial, the press runs counter to all the traditions of American justice and legal precedent. The less radical feminists see this clearly and insist that the woman's name be published when she makes the charge. Karen DeCrow, a former president of the National Organization For Women and a prominent New York attorney, insists that by shielding the woman's name the press perpetuates the view that the woman has somehow been shamed and must be protected, the very position that feminists have sought to eliminate. The shame is not hers; if anybody's it is the perpetrator, if he can be shown to be one. By calling the woman a "victim" the newspapers already assume the man is guilty, according to DeCrow, and this exacerbates the wrongs being done.[7]

DeCrow accordingly followed the *New York Times* and other reputable newspapers in publishing the name of Patricia Bowman, the woman who accused a nephew of Senator Robert Kennedy of raping her in Palm Springs after a night of heavy drinking and being picked up in a local tavern. In this case particularly, as pointed out by Ellen Goodman, the difference in male and female understandings of what constitutes rape and what does not is particularly significant. Fortunately, the jury was able to see through Bowman's story and absolved the young man based on evidence that he twice had intercourse with her and she had "massaged" him to make the second penetration possible. Had Bowman been uninterested in pursuing sexual activity with him, and familiar with Lyman's New York experience, she would have left the tavern not only sober, but alone. It is significant that the jury's verdict did nothing to satisfy the radical feminists, who then insisted that this verdict set a bad example for women who were indeed raped and came forward! In other words, these feminists insisted that whether a rape had taken place or not was not important: the jury should find the man guilty anyway! Meaning here is completely abandoned in favor of emotional outrage at the idea of rape, not at the actual incidence, and logic is abandoned in its contemplation.

The invention of date rape has given rise to a spate of misunderstandings on college campuses across the country. At Syracuse University recently a woman student accused an entire fraternity of having "gang raped" her. (She later admitted to having invented the story.) Subsequently a radical feminist student placed posters upon campus buildings, printed handbills, and painted graffiti on sidewalks, blaming the fraternity for the (nonexistent) gang rape. The fraternity complained to the university administration of this slander. A hearing was held by the university judiciary board and the woman was found guilty and placed on academic probation. This roused the ire of local radical feminists, who raided the administration building and sought to transform the story into a date rape acquittal.[8] The illogic here, particularly as it occurred on a university campus, did not go without notice, but the press emphasized the date-rape aspect although it was admittedly false, rather than the slander aspect, thus misinforming its readership and catering to the salacious date-rape mania of the public. The emotional response was thus similar to that in the Kennedy-Bowman case.

Once a discourse on rape is undertaken, false accusations of rape become more frequent. In one Syracuse neighborhood, a woman reported that her boyfriend raped her and had him arrested. A few days later she admitted that he had not, but that she was angry with him for having gone out one night without her and had decided to punish him. In another case Ann Hall told deputies she was kidnapped, raped, and assaulted by a knife-wielding stranger. The county spent a considerable amount of time and money attempting to trace the rapist but could find nothing. She finally confessed to having invented the story and was subsequently charged. "She is the second local woman in four weeks to be charged with falsely reporting a rape," the local newspaper noted.[9] This is in addition to the one who had decided to "punish" her boyfriend for seemingly neglecting her. More recently Susan Murphy extorted $450 from an innocent neighbor who scarcely knew her by threatening to claim he had raped her. So outrageous had the practice become of reporting names of the males but not the females in the newspaper accounts and presuming the male guilty, that the frightened man agreed to make three payments of $150 each to Murphy. When the man's sister learned from her brother what had happened, she notified the police, and Murphy and a confederate were arrested. "In a statement to police, Murphy admitted to lying."[10] So pervasive is the media practice of identifying the accused man but not the woman "victim" that often, when the accusation proves false, her name is still withheld. A recent (July 30, 1992) newspaper account illustrates this:

A County Court jury deliberated about seven hours last Thursday before finding Bartholomew Smith innocent of first degree rape, first degree sexual abuse, third degree criminal possession of a weapon.

Smith, 22, of Delaware Street, was freed from jail after spending seven months behind bars. He was accused of entering the woman's Brighton Avenue apartment and raping her.

The prosecution presented no physical evidence that the woman was raped, Bartholomae (Smith's lawyer) said. The only real evidence against Smith was the woman's testimony that he raped her, Bartholomae said.[11]

In contemporary American society there are many neurotic women and many neurotic men, and neurosis is often associated with sexual tensions and proclivities. Differential gender socialization in American society has repressed the sexual desires of many of its women, and in periods such as this we can expect the verbalization of all kinds of neurotic fantasies and the performance of all kinds of neurotic behaviors. Rape "fantasies" were dismissed by earlier feminists as kinds of whitewashes, together with penis envy and other Freudian insights into female behaviors in repressive societies. But the near hysterical reactions of radical feminists to rape stories lends credence to the fantasy theory and their blatant attempts to co-opt everything male certainly reinforces the penis-envy thesis. Reasonable feminists such as Goodman, DeCrow, Landers, and others do not exhibit this hysteria in their writing. But even a casual reading of what passes for "feminist theory" or attendance at any radical feminist rally discloses a preoccupation with what appears to be perceived as the biological injustice of being "cursed" not only with menstruation but with childbirth, coupled to a rage at anything masculine, be it logic, religion, philosophy, history, or indifference to what is perceived as the female plight in life. Having sought to convince themselves and others that the female and male sexual experiences are identical, that sex is an accident of "plumbing" that has nothing to do with "gender," they are outraged at rape since it blatantly negates such claims. A man can rape a woman (or a man), but a woman cannot sexually rape a man (or a woman). In the few cases where women have been legally convicted of sexual rapes it is because they assisted men in holding down their female victims or otherwise participated in a male-directed ritual. Thus, the radical feminist notion of sexual equality beats its head against the wall on the matter of rape: he can do, sexually, what she cannot. This only further confounds the confusion created by the insistence that rape is not sexual in nature, but a crime of violence, and that, however, it has nothing to do with violence, only with whether a man understands what a woman truly means when she says yes or no. And that she must not be identified but he must be.

That such a contradictory position is irrational is immediately apparent. It would be wrong, however, to neglect the historical context of this contradiction and its roots in Western society generally. Sexual activity is nonrational activity: it is, in terms of the classical Parsons-Bales model of language and society, *emotive-expressive*, rather than *instrumental* activity.[12] This was appreciated by the Calvinistic Puritans, who emphasized reason as the truly god-given gift to man. It was this emphasis on the rational that led Puritan John Milton to champion freedom of the press, and Puritan Isaac Newton to champion the pursuit of scientific explanation. The American sociologist Robert K. Merton has shown how seventeenth-century Puritanism led to the development of medicine and other scientific technologies,[13] and the whole matter of this rational bent has been explored by the German sociologist Max Weber in what has become a series of classical studies of the Protestant ethic and the spirit of capitalism.[14] Reason, and reason alone, was to govern all human behaviors, according to the rationalistic Calvinism the Puritans exemplified. This is basic sociology, widely taught.

The principal reason we associate sexual taboos with "Puritanism" is because it was in the sexual that the Puritans found the irrational element that might contradict their purely rational pursuits. Sexual activity is emotive, irrational activity. True, we are enjoined by the very Bible the Puritans championed to "be fruitful and multiply." This is a duty imposed upon us. Thus, sexual activity oriented to procreation may be necessary. But, the Puritans reasoned, since it is irrational activity and, therefore, beneath our highest nature, we must not enjoy it or employ it for pleasure-seeking purposes. It is something necessary, like excretion and hunger. The unpardonable sins are therefore those of the glutton, the coprophile, the drunkard, and sensualist. Hester Prynne wears the scarlet letter of shame because she so enjoyed the sexual that she performed it out of wedlock, something reprehensible to the Puritan.

Thus, Puritan rationality demanded an avoidance of sexual

activity, and indulged in it only for procreation, since, as Saint Paul had earlier warned, it is "better to marry than to burn," and a woman must cover her head of hair in church lest "the angels, looking down, be corrupted." Corruption and sexuality were part and parcel of the same irrationality in the Puritan nexus.

Max Weber attempted to show how this insistence on wholly rational activity has been a continuing process in the West. The nonrational or irrational pose threats to our understanding of how the world "ought" to be ordered, whether it is in fact so ordered or not. Following Nietzsche, Weber pointed to the prevalent tendency in the West to cover up or deny the irrational aspect of human behaviors by substituting rational explanation. More recently Michel Foucault and others have shown how this is so in the invention of psychiatric "disorders," in verbal definitions of crimes and related activities, including the sexual. This is often concealed beneath or within the intricacies of language. In language we cope with the impossibility of conveying to another that which we intend, or that which we suppose we intend, or think that we might intend. But our understanding of that which we suppose we intend is derived not from any absolute reality, but as Karl Mannheim, the Hungarian sociologist appreciated earlier,[15] from contending and conflicting ideological positions; each of which seeks to impose its definitions upon us and upon others for the power interests of the groups espousing them. Feminists desire more power, as do democrats, zionists, republicans, capitalists, communists, catholics and protestants, and any other ideological group one may name. I have discussed this elsewhere.[16] In the present instance it is not simply the power demands that attract our attention, coupled as they are to legalistic definitions of victimizations and attempts to define new categories of victims among those proposing the definitions; it is the sociological phenomenon of the continuing effort to suppress the passionate and irrational aspect of certain activities by offering new definitions that increasingly deny any connection with passion or the irrational. This has been explored by Foucault in his *Discourse on Language*.[17] More recently, Steven Seidman has traced the irrational fear of the consequences of sexual impulses through Victorian into modern times and shown how this was accompanied by attempts to reconfigure the relationship between sex, love, and marriage.[18]

The invention of date rape masks the fear of the unpredictable that lies at the heart of the passionate. A woman in a compromising situation seeks to "be in control" of that which may not be controllable. It is one more desperate attempt to be able to predict the unpredictable, to retain control, and not succumb to passionate activity that may take charge of us and overwhelm us. It encourages a desperate appeal to the rational (no means no) in the face of the irrationality of sexual behavior, an attempt to deprive it of its passion. It, therefore, is not the rape, but the sexual activity that disrupts the equanimity of the protesters. Although to many a nonpassionate orgasm may be unimaginable, to others orgasms represent an intrusive and unwelcome loss of control over one's own behavior in an interactional situation. When this is coupled to the opposition to the masculine that is typical of so much radical feminist rhetoric, it signifies this loss of control as a consequence of activities of the enemy, the male. This can be seen as an overwhelming emotional defeat, and from this ideological position it must therefore be avoided at all costs. True rape (in which orgasm by the female is highly unlikely) becomes the symbolic substitute for submission to the male generally. In the war of the sexes, lampooned in *New Yorker* cartoons by James Thurber and others in more relaxed times, so-called date rape becomes a principal weapon in the arsenal of those devoted to destruction of everything deemed "patriarchal," which is to say, everything male.

This violent abuse of both the concept of rape and of the word itself constitutes a rape of the very idea of rape. It is a violent assault on language and interaction that seeks to transform the meaning of a word while retaining the cathexis, the emotional power, the word carries with it. By pretending that the word applies only to wholly rational activity, date rape definitional proponents seek to shield their mentalities from the horror of the unpredictable, and hence participate in a social process well at work in the history of the West at least from the early 1600s. Whereas the earlier Puritans set the sexual aside as irrational and therefore beneath human dignity, our latter-day puritans appear oblivious of the nature of their own puritanism and have seized upon the concept of rape as a kind of verbal weapon to conceal their horror at their own vulnerability: their susceptibility to human passion.

Social activity between individuals, of whatever kind, is interactional activity, always reciprocally involving more than one self. Persons interact with each other on the basis of learned behaviors and coping mechanisms acquired through their socialization. Such socialization must be distinguished from education: the latter is instrumental, planned activity, the former is often unobtrusive and emotive-expressive; instrumental activity is fairly easy to transmit, via books, maps, and other educational means. Socialization is less easily defined or controlled: it seeps in during our childhood and is the sum of scarcely understood happenings and observations we often unconsciously perform. In our childhood we tend to accept these influences unthinkingly; in adolescence we try to resist them unless they come from others like ourselves, and in adulthood we attempt to synthesize them all into a meaningful pattern. If we succeed in this attempt, traditional teaching says we may be led to wisdom, not simply to knowledge. Both education and socialization take place against a background of our irrational fears, anxieties, and doubts, all of which may have roots in our animal nature but which have, via our socialization, been imbued with symbolic meanings. Thus, symbolic meanings are implicit in the concepts of wisdom and knowledge. In language we may seek to encode these meanings; but no two languages are identical: they, too, are cultural products that determine other cultural products, and that persist by reproducing themselves. Contemporary sociologists call such systems, capable of reproducing and referencing themselves, *autopoietic*.[19]

In American society, as in societies generally, there are many distinct cultures: cultural homogeneity no longer exists in the world. In America the problem is acute; America is a pluralistic society made up of many races, religions, ethnic backgrounds and dissimilarities. That men and women are differentially socialized in American society has long been known, and has been the subject of humor and of a playful "war between the sexes" until fairly recently. But this is too-simplistic a conceptualization.

Black women in the United States, for example, may have little in common with white women, or the poor white with the white middle classes. This realization has slowly grown on a number of groups. In 1990, for example, the black women's caucus resigned from the Womens' Studies Association because the latter, with its predominantly white middle-class radical feminist biases, had nothing whatever to do with the problems faced by black women in American society. The notion that because individuals have biological properties in common they must have social problems in common is only one more appeal to the rational that scarcely masquerades the irrationality at its core. Social problems are generated in the social, not the biological nexus. Most black women in the United States (and elsewhere) face different problems from white women because of their different social contexts. A former colleague of mine, an African Moslem woman, teaching Womens Studies in a downstate college, confesses to being outraged at the suggestion that African women (for example) have the identical problems as white middle-class American women, and that common biology is the most salient factor in determining their social problems.

Cultural diversity can contribute significantly to a society's growth and development. Racial or gender tensions exacerbate real and imaginary differences, creating stereotypes that generally demean their proponents rather than those they attack. The raping of the concept of rape exacerbates the increasing fracturing of American society, accentuates division by creating imaginary as well as real situations to intensify the traditional "war between the sexes." It uses fear of the irrational to augment irrational fears. That in doing so it is symptomatic of a general phenomenon in what has been called "the decline of the West" does not make it more tolerable: it simply increases the bars of the iron cage of rationality that others have pointed out to us. It does not liberate us, male or female: it only further imprisons us in our incomprehension of ourselves and others, and confounds us with its dilution of meanings.

NOTES

1. The Anita Hill affair is typical of this thirst for the salacious, pandered to by the media. A black woman attorney sought to intrude

upon the nomination of a black male Supreme Court justice because (she claimed) many years before he had made some off-color remarks in her presence. All television networks seized upon airing the hearings live because of the sex talk that characterized it. The nomination was nevertheless approved.

2. Deborah Tannen's 1990 book, *You Just Don't Understand: Women and Men in Conversation*, published by William Morrow and Company, was denounced as sexist by some feminists because it asserted a difference between men and women.

3. Ellen Goodman is a widely syndicated Boston-based columnist who writes from a feminist perspective. This article appeared in the May 3, 1991, issue of the Syracuse *Post Standard*.

4. According to the News Service Reports, "Dunn, a three time Grammy nominee and the daughter of a Church of Christ minister said, 'I've always considered myself a feminist,' " but Leah Aldridge claimed "the song truly does send the wrong message that women don't know what they want."

5. Ann Landers, "Advice: Physical Signs Should Tell Women When To Yell 'Stop.' " Syndicated column.

6. The High Impact Cities program was conducted employing National Crime Panel, rather than Uniform Crime Reports, data on criminal victimization in selected cities. I conducted the analysis and supervised the data reduction for the City of Newark, New Jersey.

7. Karen DeCrow, "Naming Names." *The Syracuse New Times*, May 8, 1991.

8. "Student On Academic Probation For Fliers Alleging Frat Rape." Syracuse *Post Standard*, April 26, 1991.

9. "Woman Charged with Falsifying Rape Story." Syracuse *Post Standard*, May 31, 1991.

10. "Woman Accused in Extortion Scam." Syracuse *Post Standard*, July 25, 1991.

11. "County Jury Clears Man Accused of Raping Acquaintance." Syracuse *Post Standard*, July 30, 1992.

12. Talcott Parsons and Robert F. Bales were colleagues at Harvard who developed models of social situations and societies based upon small group experiments employing the coding of language acts. The two principal dimensions in the Bales Interaction Process Analysis are *instrumental activity* and *expressive-emotive activity*. Although the seminal work of Parsons and Bales is either unknown or ignored by Deborah Tannen (see note two), it too shows male and female differences in use and understanding of language. Male language and activity tends to be instrumental; female language emotive expressive (integrative). A

model of the family was posited based upon these and related differences and similarities. See George V. Zito, *The Sociology of Shakespeare* (New York: Peter Lang), 1991, for an application of this method to literary (Shakespearean and other Elizabethan) works and a discussion of the model and method.

13. Robert K. Merton, *Science and Technology in Seventeenth Century England* (New York: Harper and Row), 1970.

14. Max Weber's monumental project was not limited to the origins of modern western capitalism and its association with developments within Calvinistic protestantism, however, but explored the peculiar position rationality held in the development of Western society.

15. See Karl Mannheim, *Ideology and Utopia* (New York: Harcourt Brace and Ward), 1939.

16. See Zito, 1983, 123ff.

17. Included as an appendix in *The Archaeology of Knowledge* (New York: Harper and Row), 1972.

18. Steven Seidman, *Romantic Longings: Love in America, 1830–1980* (New York: Routledge), 1991. Seidman is especially sensitive to the irrationality in the "new morality" that seeks to censor "pornography" while preaching "sexual liberation."

19. See Niklas Luhmann, *Ecological Communication* (Chicago: University of Chicago Press), 1989. In connection with erotic phenomena, see his *Love As Passion* (Cambridge, Mass.: Harvard University Press), 1986.

Chapter 6 _____

The Rise and Fall of the JAP

There are newly coined words with newly coined meanings that are difficult to decode or translate, and these too throw the whole matter of meaning itself into doubt and confusion. We can see this most clearly in words that come into usage to designate particular types of things, without at the same time specifying the salient characteristics constituting the thing the word seeks to designate. This is a well-known linguistic process and is not new. However, in their attempts to impose their definitions in place of culturally inherited ones, adult groups often invent words, as teenagers do, and see them finally taken over by the "out group" or by the general public in an attempt to neutralize or sanitize the original meaning, or to substitute a new one.

With the increase in enrollments in the late 1960s and early 1970s a personality type began to emerge in East Coast colleges and universities, particularly at places such as Boston University, Syracuse University, and branches of the University of Florida. Quickly designated by Jewish and non-Jewish students alike as "the JAP," an acronym for *J*ewish *A*merican *P*rincess, the type lasted only a few years, and due to peer pressure in the use of the acronym in a proscriptively negative sense, quietly disappeared. Attempts to extend the acronym to Jewish males (substitute prince for princess) and even to Roman Catholics (substitute RCP) were less successful and never made substantial headway.

The JAP of the late 1960s and early 1970s became a target for ridicule for her lack of good taste. These young women, apparently unaware of the accepted norms of their classmates, were not only overdressed and over-jewelled—adorned with redundant gold chains and heavily perfumed—they were a generally unacceptable student type to both peers and many of the faculty. Such persons almost always sat in the last rows of lecture halls and classrooms, chewing gum, applying polish to their fingernails, and conversing with other JAPs. This often interfered with classroom decorum to the point where professors would feel compelled to interrupt their lectures and demand silence. On other occasions, the offending females were ordered out of the room or lecture hall. Their exaggerated protests and feigned indignation did little to mollify the general feelings against them. Who first coined the term JAP remains a mystery; these students were far too young to have been influenced by the negative connotations of the term as used in World War II for the Japanese. Indeed, at the time, when questioned, the students I interviewed could not understand why *Jap* was understood as a term of opprobrium for the Japanese, since it simply abbreviated their name. They associated the term only with these young women, and were unaware of its earlier usage. Applied to classroom JAPs, however, the negative cathexis was always evident. JAPs were females to be shunned, except by other JAPs. Less ostentatious young Jewish women were embarrassed by them, and were quick to dissociate themselves from them. Jewish males joked about them in ways their non-Jewish classmates might hesitate to do. As in most cases, the peer pressure from their non-JAP fellow students began to have an effect on the JAPs. They grew less strident and were unable, at first, to understand what was happening. They presumed it must be somehow anti-Semitic.

When they complained to the local rabbis at their Hillel organizations, the rabbis attempted to rationalize the phenomenon for them, trying to convince them that the "goys" were labeling them because they were jealous of their high-priced clothes. This, of course, missed the point entirely and subsequently the

JAP phenomenon became sedimented as "anti-Semitism" by the local Jewish congregations. This claim quickly became diluted as the Jewish women students who did not fit this personality type continued to refer to them as JAPs. Some of their Jewish peers were spoiled rotten, they explained, particularly the women, and to call them princesses was too mild a designation, even when preceded by "Jewish American." They were simply the Jewish female version of a vulgar type that exists cross-culturally. If they were objectionable as students it was because the demographics had changed in recent years and there were more of them to be found in American universities. They had become more visible.

The peer pressure against them became too much, too strong. The JAP, as a student personality type, began to disappear from academia by the late 1970s, and they are no longer seen in classrooms. Their successors, Jewish American young women of similar ethnic and economic backgrounds, have better assimilated the current youth cultural norms than had their earlier sisters. They wear the same clothing styles as the other female students, and the same amount of jewelry. Gold chains about the neck, especially redundant chains, have largely disappeared. There was a time when virtually every female undergraduate at a university wore at least one gold chain about her neck, and the JAPs wore many; but that has gone the way of crocodile and polo horse logos. And even the students at the back of the room are quieter again, or readily squashed into silence by an academic stare from the lecturer.

Some of the overt racists found in contemporary American society later latched on to the JAP appellation, and used it indiscriminately in ethnic jokes, usually substituting it for "Kike," "Polack," "Wop," or "Nigger" in the original versions.

Most Jewish students I have interviewed do not see JAP as containing the same hatred as "Kike," or "Yid," or some of the other terms of deprecation employed by racists. And they do not understand why some ultra-sensitive Jews find the JAP term so objectionable. They recognize that it singles out a particular type of female of which they are not especially proud. Other ultra-sensitive Jews have a propensity for seeing anti-Semitism everywhere, except where it does in fact exist. Some professors have made virtual careers out of JAPism, raising the spectre of a resurgence of anti-Semitism to grab local headlines or to capitalize on speaker's fees at synagogues throughout the country. It is a curious phenomenon, since the JAP type has long since disappeared. These lecturers are not prominent scholars in their respective fields and may be compensating for a lack of expected professional recognition or similar personal reasons. They were curiously silent when JAPs were about, and only after they had disappeared did they become vocal.

The question arises, what makes such a term as JAP objectionable to those who object? And why is it acceptable to others, Jews and non-Jews alike? It must contain negative feelings of some sort: the most obvious is that the term "princess" is understood to mean "spoiled brat." There is a similar latent derogatory meaning in the American male use of the word "prince." When an American male says of another, "He is a prince," he means "He is a prick," where prick is a vulgarism for penis and has a negative cathexis associated with it. But there seems to be no sexual vulgarism associated with princess. And Jewish American is simply a designation, like Italian American or Irish American, and has no anti-Semitic property connected with it.

It may be, of course, that the early existence of the shortened word Jap, for Japanese, coupled to the vehemence with which it was pronounced by an earlier generation lent it so strong a negative connotation that youngsters picked it up from late-night war movies because of its latent inherited vehemence, so the offending young females were being compared to the male American enemies of World War II. This seems too far fetched, however: youthful cohorts tend to invent new words to encode their experience and set it apart from the experiences of previous generations: the young always seek to reinvent the world they did not create. They reject the coined words of earlier cohorts in order to draw a boundary around themselves. Moreover, the offending college females looked anything but Japanese in their garish outfits and ill manners; The Japanese are noted as a quiet, over-mannerly people. The caricature of the Japanese is one who smiles and bows and is sometimes too solicitous and over-proper, whatever his or her presumed motives: the very antithesis of the collegiate JAP. And the students I interviewed did not know of the earlier World War II usage.

Thus, although the word JAP was understood by participants to designate a particular type of college student and the type was known and readily identified by users of the term at the time, it relied primarily upon the shared cultural knowledge that "princess" was used in the derogatory sense to specify a "spoiled rotten female" rather than anything else, and that it was Jewish American versions of this that had made themselves most noticeable and objectionable in the college scene. Calling attention to the Jewish American version of the type seems to have been found uncomfortable by some Jews but not others, and some congregations campaigned to convince their members not to use the term. As already mentioned, it has generally fallen into disuse with the disappearance of the type, but remains as a vestigial appellation employed by some racists in their appetites for words others find objectionable. Indeed, the opprobrium the designated group, class, or parties find in words applied to them is in itself beyond explanation: words such as kike, wop, nigger, spic, mic and the like are not in themselves imbued with negative meanings, but nevertheless have negative feelings attributed to them, perhaps because of the vehemence with which they have been pronounced in the past by the offending persons. The invention of another such term, JAP, may be simply an indication that as denotative meanings decay and disappear, feelings are substituted as the content of words to fill the vacancy so created. Indeed, in the atmosphere of late twentieth-century America, groups identifying themselves as "victimized" see feelings as at least as legitimate as meanings in procedural programs for attaining their own ends and for redressing their grievances. This, too, contributes to the death of meaning.

Chapter 7 _____

The Politics of Images

The activities discussed in the earlier chapters all contribute to the death of meaning: the demise of holidays, the routinization of ritual in such activities as applause, the processes of defusing discourse and the confounding of meanings to the point where they become arbitrary or unknowable, as in the case of rape and JAP. The obliteration of differences among and between related but distinctly separate entities erases the only possibility of the production of meanings. Language communicates by designating differences, and it is language that by these designations encodes meanings.

Political equality arose to eliminate differences among individuals with respect to the political exercise of the franchise. But the right to vote—political equality—has become increasingly confounded with social equality. In a democratic nation political equality is paramount. But social equality has never existed in a democratic nation and probably cannot: English (and British) societies are the paramount proof of that. And the many social inequalities existing among groups in the United States, France, Switzerland, and elsewhere resist all efforts at social equality not simply because of the vested interests of privileged classes, but for fear of the void created by the removal of meanings and the consequent reduction of all values to the lowest common denominator, a process well underway in these nations.

Politicians have been quick to grasp the power unleashed by the death of meanings. This is nowhere so evident as in the case of national party platforms connected with the election of the president of the United States.

A party platform was necessary in the past to publicly publish the proposed program to be pursued by the candidate if his election should occur. Although such platforms were often specious or grandiose (or both) and candidates could not be held to them after election, they generally spelled out the long-established tenets of the party and the traditional appeals to the "American dream." What is significant from our standpoint is that such platforms constituted a set of meanings aimed at the aspirations of the voter in his or her quest for good government and a better life.

Party platforms become increasingly meaningless with respect to the outcome or pursuit of an election. Platforms, after all, are constructed of words, statements formed to establish the meanings understood by the candidate as expressing the will of the people. But with the advent of television presidential candidates (from Dwight D. Eisenhower on) have been shown to be "sold like soap," in the words of commentators: that is, they are promoted as a media commodity by visual cues and icons, not by the meanings encoded in platforms. Here the appeal of the visual has been substituted for the appeal of words, of meanings. Abraham Lincoln could not be elected president in the video age for the same reason that John F. Kennedy and Bill Clinton were: the visual portrayal of the physical. The visual has taken precedence over the politically meaningful. Only in such an iconographic jungle could a second-rate movie actor such as Ronald Reagan (who had difficulty even remembering his lines) be elected as president of the United States. Only after the death of meanings, when voting became devoid of meaning, could a George Bush acquire the position. This was clearly expounded by the conservative columnist George Will in a widely syndicated column appearing July 30, 1992, three months before the election: "the Bush campaign, like Bush himself, uses words not to convey meaning but as audible confetti . . . When Perot withdrew,

Bush's people promptly praised him as 'wise' and 'courageous'. To them, words mean nothing because nothing means anything—nothing, that is, except power or, more precisely, office." Only when meaninglessness had become the norm could Ross Perot, a politically ignorant Texas billionaire who rejected platforms and other expressions of political belief, acquire a following who believed he could become president only because he had the money to manipulate the media into campaigning for him. However, in the iconographic jungle of the politics of the 1990s, his physical appearance gradually worked against his ambitions rather than his political deficiencies: his appearance was compared to Frank Perdue, a homely chicken breeder who lampooned himself in his TV ads.

It has not gone unnoticed that political campaigning has shifted away from oratory and written platforms, away from words and meanings, to video promotions featuring visual appeals. This is now taken for granted. The campaign of Bill Clinton in 1992 was carefully constructed as a series of video events, with pop-cultural icons and rhetorics. In the famous TV debate between Nixon and Kennedy, political commentators noted that Kennedy triumphed over Nixon because Nixon *looked* unshaven and ill at ease, while Kennedy *looked* clean-cut, sanitary. In 1988 Dukakis looked too short, even small on the TV screen, and the Bush campaign against him relied on this and other negative visual icons—the obvious pollution of Boston Harbor, an unsavory-looking black criminal parolee, and the like. In the 1992 presidential campaign, Bill Clinton, a baby-boomer of the TV generation, had a clear iconographic advantage over the radio-nurtured George Bush, who did not know how to handle either the questioners or his fellow TV performers on camera. A platform, as such, was not presented as part of the campaign. Instead, a series of negative images featuring the opponent formed the principle elements of the election appeal of the candidates.

Erving Goffman has noted that it is appearance, rather than competence, that now makes one socially acceptable. Goffman terms this willful manipulation of appearance, *symptomatic behavior,* since audiences now judge performances of all kinds as staged performances.[1] The judgment is based upon appearances, rather than competence or substance. In American politics symptomatic behavior has reached its fullest on-stage development.

Membership in a group identified by ascription, rather than achievement, is becoming a political norm. Although John F. Kennedy had cautioned, in accepting the Democratic nomination for president, that people should not vote for him or against him simply because of his Roman Catholic religion, an ascribed characteristic, in the 1992 political campaign, women candidates such as Diane Feinstein dispensed with political proclamations of any kind and presented themselves to voters only on the basis of being female, also an ascribed condition, and publicly proclaimed a determination not to present any "position" statements that of necessity would involve a commitment to meanings. Ross Perot had similarly declined to make any "position" statements, so whatever political ideas, if any, such candidates held were not offered for consideration by voters. Texans, however, like women, come in all varieties, and there is no telling what one is getting by their outward characteristics.

The decline of meanings in the political arena brings about a frantic search for possible definitions at the very time definitions are most vulnerable and subject to haphazard change. Thus, black Americans have, within a span of perhaps twenty years, sought desperately to find a noun or phrase that would identify themselves to their own satisfaction and differentiate them from other Americans without losing sight of the rights and privileges they believe they are entitled to. The chronology of the nomenclature is itself illuminating. Starting from the earlier designation as *colored* (as in the National Association for the Advancement of Colored People), a progression of terms followed annually: *negro, Black, black, Black American, Afro-American, African American,* and finally (at least by 1992) *person of color,* the last a wholly meaningless designation, since all persons have color except albinos (and even they are seldom completely lacking in melanin). The attempt to impose meanings upon meaninglessness is clear: colored (the earlier designation) had suffered as a designation as a consequence of what had happened in South Africa and other racist environments, and it also brought to mind the NAACP, primarily a working-class organization of blacks rather than the professional-class organization typified by the Urban

League and the developing black bourgeoisie in the United States. The misnomer, persons of color, however, emphasized the black citizen as a *person,* a much sought-after designation by the hitherto disenfranchised minority; a term such as black person, on the other hand, would have compromised the notion of the person by conditioning it. At any event, the new designation is avoided by any but the most affluent black Americans and cannot be expected to last since it is cumbersome and, since everyone is a "person of one color or another" completely meaningless. One cannot be a person and lack color.

The black writer, Shelby Steele, in an article entitled "The New Sovereignty,"[2] points out that the "push for equality among groups necessarily made for an inequality among individuals that prepared the ground for precisely the racial, gender, and ethnic divisiveness that, back in the sixties, we all said we wanted to avoid," and notes that each resulting Affirmative Action and entitlement program, "has most helped those who least need it— white middle-class women and the black middle class. Poor blacks do not guide the black grievance groups. Working-class women do not set NOW's agenda." The political expediency of such programs as Affirmative Action, where membership in a self-defined "victim" group entitles one to an advantage over others otherwise more qualified than oneself, even if one has not oneself been victimized, made constitutional guarantees of the equality of persons meaningless. Attempts to correct past wrongs to members of a designated group by conferring competitive advantages to present members of that group clearly discriminates against nonmembers of the group. This became clearly evident to me when a former graduate student of mine whose Ph.D. dissertation defense I had directed was denied a position on a faculty that was awarded to a woman who had only a Master's degree in this area and was "working toward a Ph.D." The excuse given by the administration was that they had to hire more women and blacks to satisfy Affirmative Action demands, even when it involved hiring a less-than-qualified person simply because she was a woman. Ten years later, the woman is tenured on that faculty and is still "working toward a Ph.D."

The absence of meanings brings about the absence of academic standards. Grade inflation at the college and university levels

automatically follows. Incompetent persons, scarcely profession-
als, are placed in positions where they can do damage. The
quality of instruction and the overall quality of professors and
teachers decline following a kind of Gresham's Law, where bad
teachers drive out good teachers. College courses today are re-
treads of what high-school courses were fifteen years ago. College administrators, confronted with shrinking budgets and
declining enrollments as demographic changes make themselves
felt, apply subtle and less-than-subtle pressures on faculty to
minimize failing grades and simplify requirements. Department
chairs slavishly relay such administration demands to the faculty.
Such "chairpersons" are in continual battles with the shrinking
number of faculty who attempt to maintain traditional academic
standards, threatening and cajoling them so that "student enrollments do not drop and we are not penalized by the dean
and chancellor" as a consequence of awarding failing grades to
students who do not meet course requirements. This has become
a dominant theme in professional society meetings throughout
the country, where academics informally meet between sessions
to discuss "what's happening" at their colleges or universities.

A professor known to me, spending a semester abroad in an
American university's overseas program, was verbally harassed
by his American chairwoman, via long-distance telephone calls,
for failing students who did not attend classes and did not turn
in the required course work. On his return to the States she
continued the harassment and warned him that "students would
not take the course if they knew there was the possibility of
failing, and the university's program would be jeopardized."

The situation confronting American blacks in their attempt at
self-identification is mirrored in that confronting American Indians. The attempted substitution of "Native American" for "Indian," proposed by some, is similarly meaningless. Anyone born
in America is a "native American," not a naturalized American.
The word *indian* means "dark person"; that is why the natives
of the subcontinent were called "indians" by Indo-Europeans
with lighter colored skin than themselves; that is why india ink
is black, by the way, not because it comes from India (it does not
and never has). When the navigators of fifteenth- and sixteenth-
century Italy, Portugal, and Spain referred to the inhabitants of

the New World as indians it was because they were people of a color darker than themselves, not because they thought they had found India.

The term "Native American" has been rejected by some Indian groups. Randy John, a member of the Seneca Nation of Indians of New York State and a professor at St. Bonaventure University near the Salamanca Indian Reservation south of Buffalo, New York, is an ardent researcher on American Indian affairs. He serves on several committees of the Seneca Nation of Indians and claims the term "Native American" is meaningless, since it groups into one collective assortment Aleuts, Eskimos, the Indians of the Northwest, the Plains Indians, Indians of the Southwest, and others who share no common cultural identity and who have widely different problems. The Kwakiutl of British Columbia, for example, with their ancient potlatches and totem poles have nothing in common with the long-house Indians of the eastern forests or the tent-dwelling buffalo hunters of the central plains or the pueblo dwellers of Arizona and New Mexico.

The American *Indian* Movement that came to prominence with Wounded Knee and the Pine Ridge episodes identified itself not as "Native American"—perhaps seeing the generic application of that term to the very oppressors they sought to oppose. Indeed, even the use of the word American, the adjective form of the name of the Italian mapmaker Amerigo Vespucci, challenges the efforts at ethnic distinction by use of such nomenclature.

The need for an identification as a member of an "outsider" or "victimized" group has become prominent as the meanings of words and phrases become less precise. In the United States, women are still struggling for a word or phrase to identify themselves as a group. Such organizations as the National Organization of Women (NOW) remain confounded by the necessity of keeping the *-men* in *women*. After the desperate effort to have *person* substituted for *man* in such words as chairman, as discussed earlier, and in mailman, fireman, and the like, the problem of Women in the organization's name is a continuing embarassment. *Woperson* clearly will not do, as it restates the prejudicial notion of women as complainers, woe-persons. The feminist emphasis upon changing or challenging the meaning of words un-

favorable to themselves has had other embarrassing consequences. The now-defunct Equal Rights Amendment, championed vigorously by NOW and other feminist organizations as
the coined acronym ERA, has at last disappeared as an issue,
leaving ERA as the name of a laundry detergent and the icons
associated with it in TV advertising.

The failure of the Equal Rights Amendment, the Supreme
Court's support of the Pennsylvania approach to abortion leg-
islation, the failure of Geraldine Ferraro to garner votes as a
vice-presidential candidate, the failure of Anita Hill to preclude
the installation of Judge Thomas to the bench, the Kennedy
rapeless "date rape," and similar post-feminist era failures have
rendered the efforts of such organizations as NOW archaic and
unproductive, and their efforts to dominate definitions of situations increasingly unlikely. In the political arena such efforts
have been further challenged by the failures of women elected
to positions of power: Margaret Thatcher in Britain, forced by
her party to step down because of her incompetence; Mrs.
Ghandi in India, surely the author of the most repressive regime
in that country's history; Corazón Aquino's well-intentioned but
completely ineffectual rule in the Philippines. Other women of
great accomplishment—Mother Theresa and Sally Ride, for example—are altogether ignored by such organizations as NOW
since they do not fit the anti-male, "genderless" or lesbian interests of the foundering "movement."

Once gender was injected into political matters, the traditional
meaning base became obscured. A thing, a position, a candidacy
was not what it was by virtue of the meanings associated with its
duties, obligations, accomplishments, and privileges; it was made
a reflection of sex, irrespective of its genderless meanings. Something similar occurred in the arts. In an article entitled "And If
You Play 'Bolero' Backwards," Edward Rothstein of the *New York
Times* noted that

During a discussion about Schubert's homosexuality recently at the 92d
Street Y, the musicologist Susan McClarey suggested ways in which the
second movement of Schubert's "Unfinished" Symphony resembled
contemporary gay literature. Hearing her made me nostalgic for old-
fashioned formalist criticism—no muss, no fuss; just name the chords,

describe the structure, and listen. Her suggestion, casually linking arts separated by more than 160 years and a chasm of ideologies, also made me feel sympathy for an audience member who later asked, with dead-pan seriousness, whether members of the panel thought Schubert's being short and fat affected his music.

Here an assortment, a multitude of musical meanings was re-jected in favor of one singular sexual meaning. This phenom-enon is similar to what we have seen in our discussion of applause. As with applause, a single response is furnished ir-respective of the nature of the occasion. A new distinguishing meaning is not furnished; instead, the old distinguishing mean-ing is destroyed and the differences among things made to ap-pear insignificant. A thing is, after all, what it is by its exclusion of the things it differs from, not by its commonality with other things. The meaning of a thing lies in language, and language is a system that works by exclusion and differences.[3]

The identification problem confronting American Indians, American blacks, and American women, in terms of language, now also plagues American Jews. The matter of the JAP has already been discussed. Here it is worth noting that, with the emergence of the State of Israel and the flowering of Islamic protest in the Middle East, the immigration into the United States of Arabs and other Semitic-language peoples has markedly in-creased. The American Jewish population, on the other hand, has continually declined as intermarriage with Christians and others has continued to rise. *Anti-Semitism,* as a designating word and concept, has accordingly lost most of its meaning. The term arose at a time when Jews constituted the principle Semitic-language group in the United States and faced discrimination in many social and political areas. With the rise in importance of the Arab states, especially those that produce and export oil, on the international scene, such a term as anti-Semitic has be-come increasingly meaningless. Arabs now constitute the prin-ciple Semitic-language group, not Jews. Should not the antagonisms being experienced by many Arab immigrants to the United States, similar to that faced by earlier Jews, be classified as anti-Semitism? In short, the monopoly on the term previously maintained by the Jewish segment of the U.S. population has become meaningless. Most "Semites" in the world are Arabs, not Jews. The charge of being "anti-Semitic" has lost most of its power.

As Shelby Steele points out, the displacement of individual rights by group rights ends by pitting one group against all others where the group perceives itself as "victimized." This victim-mania has infiltrated many areas of American society: individuals claim to be victims of alcoholism because their parents were, to be wife beaters or child abusers because their fathers were, and so on, ad infinitum and ad nauseam. Coalescing into groups for political posturing, they then make demands for favored treatment over others and sometimes get them, as in Affirmative Action and other entitlements. But in the process they render the meanings associated with individual responsibility and autonomy irrelevant, and these meanings grow dim at first and finally disappear entirely. The individual, as an entity, ceases to be important and the group alone is seen as significant. In the frantic search for possible self-identification and consequent self-hood as a group they inadvertently contribute to the destruction of the meaning of the self and augment the already deteriorating condition they sought to redress. They too, contribute to the death of meaning.

NOTES

1. Erving Goffman, *The Presentation of Self in Everyday Life* (New York, Anchor), 1959.
2. Shelby Steele. 1992. "The New Sovereignty." *Harper's* 285 (1706).
3. See de Saussure, 1959.

Chapter 8

Maiming Messages

There is an additional source of destruction of meaning that we might not expect unless we have had inadvertent "hands on" experience with it. Written language has always been a function of the technology of its time, from the sharpened stylus engraving cuneiform strokes on soft clay tablets in Akkad and Sumer through quill and ink, to fountain pens and then typewriters. Innovations in the materials of writing have played significant roles in the kinds of discourse that could be expressed and the consequent production of readable texts. Marshal McLuhan's *Guttenberg Galaxy* reminds us of the transformation in meanings brought about by the printing press. Although the notion that "the medium is the message" is not as salient today as in 1962 when introduced by McLuhan, this decline is due at least in part to the rapidly increasing incomprehensibility of all messages.

This book, like many others these days, was written on a personal computer employing a word processor program. Brought up on typewriters, most authors have an initial difficulty in making the transition to the computer-based manuscript procedures, but the benefits are great, and it takes only a little effort to master the applicable techniques. In revision and moving pieces of text about, italicizing, and keeping neat margins and the like (as well as benefitting from having built-in spelling checkers, thesauri, hyphenation programs, and other aids), the introduction of word processing programs has been a boon to writing and to writers. I use WordPerfect 5.1 on an IBM/DOS (disk operating system) clone, and have written my last three books on this machine. However, when I co-authored a book with my wife, and in my last book as well, there was a need for diagrams and charts to explain many of the concepts. I did not hesitate to borrow a Macintosh computer and associated software from my university to create the needed diagrams. Devoted as I am to the IBM/MSDOS for its mastery of text, I freely conceded that in the area of graphics, the Macintosh is truly superior. With the programs known as MacDraw or MacPaint, for example, one can draw very accurate diagrams with lines that meet at true right angles when required and with type faces (fonts) that are whatever size and style one desires. One can execute these designs quickly and repeatedly, and the associated printer, although not a laser style device, takes one's efforts and transforms them into a beautiful printed page.

Having prepared several dozen different "Figures" (explanatory diagrams or schematic representations) for these books and liking the results, I was tempted to try writing manuscript text on a Macintosh but found the effort peculiarly frustrating and unsatisfactory. I finally returned the computer to the university and went back to writing on my IBM clone. I had decided that the reason I did not like the Macintosh for writing was the small size of the screen. But now I am not so sure that was the real reason.

The IBM/MSDOS and the Macintosh have different operating systems: that is, the internal programming is arranged quite differently and requires different responses from users to obtain similar results. Both systems are "user friendly" but users differ. It is perhaps inevitable that some people would find one set of responses more desirable than the other and accordingly favor that particular machine. However, this is only part of the explanation for my difficulty with the Macintosh when it comes to doing anything other than using it to draw figures and diagrams. I was at a loss to understand my problem with text on the Macintosh until I read an article by Marcia Peoples Halio in the

January 1990 issue of the journal *Academic Computing*. Then it all made sense, and the sense it made lends additional weight to the analysis presented in these chapters.

The IBM/MSDOS system[1] requires that the user type in the word commands he or she wishes to execute. To copy a file of text, for example, one must type COPY A:fn.fe B: if one wishes to copy a file from drive A (usually a "floppy disk" drive) to another disk in drive B. The name of the file (fn) is often followed by a period and an extension (fe). The file name of this chapter is MEANINGS and the extension is .CH8. The file is "stored" or retained on the floppy disk that I put into drive A, and before I write I must call it up to the screen in order for me to work on it.

By now many American office workers and other business, industrial and academic users are familiar with these procedures, but it is worth spelling out here for those who are not. The file is created by the word processor program WordPerfect, version 5.1. I have to call up the word processor program (permanently stored on my hard disk drive first, by typing its name (or WP51) and then, by selecting a certain built-in command key on the keyboard (F5) view the list of files I have, move a highlighted bar on to the line MEANINGS.CH8, press the ENTER key on the keyboard and thus have the text brought on to the screen.

With a Macintosh the procedure is quite different. I turn on the computer and wait until I see a set of pictures or schematized "icons." Some look like little pages, stacked, with titles on them. These are my files. I then move a "mouse," a little mechanical-electrical device sitting on a foam rubber pad on my desk, so that the highlight falls on the page I want, then I "click" the buttons on the mouse and the file is shown on the screen. While I am working there is a little figure of a garbage pail on the right. With my mouse I can click the button and "drag" the page over and dump it in the garbage pail, thus "trashing" it or erasing it.

In later versions of WordPerfect one may employ a mouse to "pull down" menus of commands, but although this is possible in some current programs written for use on DOS systems, in the DOS operating system itself it is not possible. In other words, if I "exit" from WordPerfect, I find myself in the DOS operating system environment. To get a list of files here I have to type DIR (for directory, the old CP/M operating system command that I grew up with) to be presented with a list of files. Then I can find a file I wish to erase and to do so, enter the command ERASE fn.ft or DEL fn.ft to erase it. There are no pictorial garbage pails in DOS. At least, there were no such icons until very recently, but let's hold off on that for the moment and return to Professor Halio.

At the University of Delaware Professor Halio had been teaching freshman composition classes for several semesters employing IBM clones. At Delaware since 1985, freshman composition classes are offered on both IBM-style machines and Macintosh machines, and students are able to choose whichever system appeals to them. They are given the same amount of training on either system, and both groups are composed of medium-skilled students with comparable levels of freshman writing ability. As at all large universities these days, there are computer clusters scattered throughout the campus that students may use for classroom purposes: to prepare reports, essays, and perhaps even take examinations.

In the spring of 1987 Halio decided to teach a composition course using Macintosh computers rather than the IBMs she had been using. "I was little prepared for the surprises that lay in wait," she writes.[2] The first batch of essays were shockers. "Never before in twelve years of teaching had I seen such a sloppy bunch of papers. Words were misspelled; commas were placed haphazardly; semicolons were virtually nonexistent.... and such fine points as quotation marks, apostrophes and question marks were treated with gay abandon." She demanded that the students take back the essays, proofread, and correct them before she would grade them. "This was a step I had not encountered with my IBMers," she remarks, and was first tempted to dismiss it as a "fluke."

But as the semester wore on she became convinced that this was no fluke. In her article she gives examples of the writing, a pop-jargon style found in advertising and teen-age media.

Although students in all sections had been given the same writing suggestions.... Mac students chose to write about such topics as fast food,

dating, bars, television, rock music, sports, relationships and phenomena such as the foam "popcorn" chips that come in so many packages.
These topics struck me as very different in a fundamental way from
the essays on capital punishment, teenage pregnancy, nuclear war and
drunk driving that I was accustomed to receiving from IBM users.

The Mac class did turn in papers that were more creatively
illustrated. She was concerned, however, by how much their
writing had been influenced by this "super friendly" operating
system. Had the student population changed? Did that account
for it? Apparently not. The following fall (1988) she was made
assistant director of the writing program at the University of
Delaware, in charge of twenty-five sections of computer-assisted
freshman composition. Without telling the instructors her sus-
picions, she asked them at the end of the semester whether they
had noticed any differences between the IBM users' papers and
the Mac users' papers. The response from the instructors was
unanimous. They stated unequivocally that students wrote worse
on the Macs, and not because they were worse writers but because
there was something about using the Mac that encouraged child-
ish vocabularies and playful use of typefaces, margins, and other
physical appearance details. Halio took twenty of the essays from
both groups and ran them through a computerized analysis program for writing, and found that Mac students wrote far fewer
complex sentences and used more "to be" verbs. They had higher
scores on weakness of prose compared to IBM users. Readability
scores on the Kincaid scale averaged 12.1 (college level) for IBM
users but only 7.95 (less than eighth grade) for Mac users.

Being an academic, Halio then reviewed the applicable literature and found that other researchers were aware that the
writing instrument could affect the cognitive process. In the
context of the studies contained in this book, the implications
are quite clear. The Macintosh uses icons and pictures to inter-
face with the user; the IBM uses words. The complexity of words
and their interrelations are the sources of meanings. Although
icons, images, pictorial representations "stand for" the meanings
of object things, they do not perform the functions that words
perform. Words get their meanings from, are defined by other
words, not by things. Video games in arcades frequented by

adolescents and children capitalize upon such icons and avoid the complexity of words precisely because words involve meanings and meanings involve even greater complexity; the immature lack the ability to decipher complex meanings. Video arcade games are part and parcel of the adolescent's search for meaningless "fun" of any kind.

Halio is vaguely suspicious that students approach the Macintosh, with its icon-driven system, much as they approach video games: a fun thing, not something for serious work and effort. This may indeed be part of the problem, but if it is, it is related directly to the absence of meanings that liberates the "fun" endeavors. The demand for instant gratification rejects any appeal to meanings: it is *pleasure* oriented, not *thought* oriented. Like so many other contemporary efforts, its appeal is to the emotional rather than the rational. "Fun" calls for emotional elation rather than ratiocination. It is directed to the moment, to the *Now* at all costs.

The super user-friendly emotional appeal of the iconic glyph is powerful, that is why there is so much permanence in religious symbols and iconography of all kinds. So strong is the appeal of the icon-driven operating system of the Mac that IBM has had to emulate it in the WINDOWS version it incorporates into its recent 486 and OS/2 (operating system #2) computers. In taking this step it is clear that IBM is joining in the decimation of meanings discussed in the previous chapters. It is aiding and abetting the decline and death of meaning. By rejecting word commands in favor of icons, it is moving away from the demotic language that enabled its own design and creation and retreating into the archaic atavism of picture language, the hieroglyphics of a growing number of essentially primitive people.

NOTES

1. IBM is the acronym for International Business Machine, the office hardware manufacturer that adapted an earlier operating system, CP/M, to its own purposes and its own machines. The earlier system employed only 64,000 bytes of memory and an ingenious system kept updating, from the temporary "floppy disks" used to store information, the amount of information taking more than the 64,000 bytes so that

this could be processed by the central control unit in the computer proper. IBM added more memory and needed an expanded version of CP/M to operate. Its greater efficiency led to increasing versions of its computers and these were "cloned" by other manufacturers. Although the earlier forms of CP/M manipulated by the Microsoft Corporation (MS) for the disk operated systems (DOS) made by IBM was available to clone users independently of IBM, their MSDOS operating system was virtually identical with subsequent IBM versions and helped proliferate the use of IBM clones in business, industry, and educational institutions.

Macintosh (Apple) did not start with CP/M and, therefore, originated an entirely different operating system. They promoted their system by giving computers to schools and requiring them to buy Macintosh programs and other software, thus creating a market that reached the school child and could influence students' later preferences. Software made for Macintosh computers cannot be used on IBM machines or its clones.

2. Marcia Peoples Halio. 1990. "Student Writing: Can the Machine Maim the Message?" *Academic Computing*, 17.

Chapter 9

Death and Taxes

Messages may get maimed in transmission as well as in decoding. But some messages are now encoded so haphazardly, or follow policy rules so arbitrary that the encoder no longer understands the intention of the rules governing their function, and the meaning of the message may become either lost or mutilated. Decoding such messages often proves impossible, and no meaning can be gleaned from them. There are times when the more shrewd entrepreneurs recognize this and take advantage of it in their manipulation of possible markets. Copy is purposely "garbled" so that the reader, no longer skilled at decoding messages in the new iconographic environment, can misread what is required or what he or she is being offered. The proliferation of "million dollar" awards as a consequence of one having been "selected" in some make-believe lottery have flooded newspaper pages. Hardly a week goes by when a notice is not received in the mail that one has won some glorious prize, and all one need do is contact the phone number listed to find which of the many possible prizes one has already secured. Very careful reading is required to learn that one has, indeed, won nothing at all thus far, but further participation is required for the person to learn how and where the award (if any) may be granted. These mailings, many of which are outright frauds and few, if any, involve

Table 2

```
                    Central Cape Dodge
              Hyannis, Massachusetts 02610
                     PASSENGER VEHICLES
                 15,000 MILE SERVICE MENU
                       NORMAL DRIVING
                 (15,000-45,000-75,000-ETC)
```

The following services should be maintained as stated in your
owner's manual for Severe Service. The following Service Menu
covers your required services as stated in your manual. Additional
services have been added as preventive maintenance.

	INDIVIDUAL PRICES		
	PARTS	LABOR	TOTAL
INSPECT CV BOOTS	N/C	N/C	N/C
CHANGE ENGINE OIL & FILTER	$15.14	$13.50	$28.64
LUBRICATE CHASSIS, HINGES & LOCKS	.99	4.50	5.49
SERVICE TRANSMISSION	26.66	67.50	93.16
REPPLACE FUEL FILTER* EFI	28.95	22.50	51.45
INSPECT AIR FILTER	N/C	N/C	N/C
INSPECT,CLEAN & ADJUST BRAKES	N/C	22.50	22.50
ROTATE TIRES	N/C	18.00	18.00
REPACK WHEEL BEARINGS	16.34	67.50	83.84

(The menu goes on to list other operations for a total of $397.58.
Then gives a MENU SPECIAL of $269.75)
Some models slightly higher, includes all above operations.
PRICES WILL VARY FOR REAR WHEEL DRIVE, ETC.

real awards, are by now familiar to most readers. The matter of
"garbled copy" may be less familiar. Some examples from the
interpersonal, interactional context will make this clear.

A Cape Cod woman I know purchased, in 1992, a brand new
Dodge automobile. It was her first new car, and she was thrilled
with it. She also purchased an extended-warranty package which,
she was told, would cover the costs of all oil changes, service
calls, and minor repairs, as well as the usual maintenance. She
was accordingly shocked when she received in the mail the document reproduced here (Table 2). Reading the document, she
was confused. Her owner's manual for the new vehicle stated
that at 15,000 miles she only needed an oil change and a new
oil filter. It was her understanding that this would be covered
by the warranty policy she had purchased from the dealer. But
here was an itemized list of services costing $397, which the kind-
hearted dealer had reduced to a "special" of $269.75! She was
outraged and consulted several family members and her em-
ployer to find out what she should do. They all read the material
and told her to follow what was in the owner's manual, that she

needn't use the Dodge dealer to perform these services as long as she kept a record, and that the document was simply evidence of a rip-off she could ignore. They also advised her to inform Chrysler headquarters in Michigan about the dealer's misrepresentation.

A careful reading of the "header" of this document reveals a garbled text that results in wholly meaningless communication. The header informs us the sheet covers "Passenger Vehicles" but does not tell us whether these are *all* vehicles (4 cylinder, 6 cylinder, 8 cylinder engines? station wagons? vans? front, rear, or all-wheel drive? etc.). This is the least ambiguous sentence of the header, however. We are told that this is the 15,000-mile service menu, for "normal driving," and then that this should be done in 15,000-mile increments. The next sentence begins the real obfuscation. "The following services should be maintained as stated in your owner's manual for Severe Service." But the previous sentence informed us that this was for "Normal Driving," which is not "Severe Service" but normal service. Here is a blatant contradiction. What is this menu for, really? The next sentence, in an attempt to clarify this apparent nonsense, states that, "The following Service Menu covers your required services as stated in your manual." This is an outright lie; the manual calls for changing only the oil and the oil filter. The next sentence contradicts this sentence: "Additional services have been added as preventive maintenance." Thus, having been told that what follows is from the manual, we are then told that additional nonmanual material has been added! The entire header is an incomprehensible jumble of contradictions that cannot make sense to the careful reader. Only a reader already confounded by the assault on meanings underway in American society could possibly bring their vehicle to this shop and swallow the inflated menu demands. Where only about $30 of maintenance is required at 15,000 miles by the Chrysler Corporation, this dealer seeks $269.75! Then, as if this is not bad enough, a footer tells us that the price may be even greater than this! "Prices will vary for rear-wheel drive, diesels, trucks, vans and 4-wheel drive vehicles. Service work is subject to a ten-percent hazardous waste and shop material charge not to exceed $7.50. Not valid with any other coupons or discounts."

So much for garbled information on Cape Cod. The media term for this intentional manipulation is "disinformation," itself indicative of the destruction of meaning.

A Wyoming man I know returned home with his wife and children from a trip to California, where he had visited his brothers and taken his children to Disneyland in Anaheim. "Californians are stupid," he insisted. "They've got a new sales tax and nobody knows how to figure it out, what it applies to or how much to charge." I tried explaining that any new tax poses such a problem, but he was adamant and would hear none of it. "You're missing the point," he insisted. "It's not the newness of the tax that's involved, but the simple calculation. Every place I went, from Anaheim to San Francisco, no one seemed able to perform the simplest arithmetic. I questioned some of them about where they had gone to school and found that they were at least high-school graduates and many had come out of the California college system. But they could not add or multiply the simplest numbers! I couldn't believe it." He is a member of a local Board of Education, and this experience upset him very much.

His wife, who teaches at a nearby community college, nodded in agreement. Her students do not really think, she mused, but spout ready-made answers, and tend to blame other people when their answers do not work for them. "People don't try to figure things out anymore," she said. "It's not just taxes. It's everything, from their own identities, who they are or think they are, all the way up to politics, religion and death itself. These things don't seem to mean much to them because somehow they don't look inside themselves for answers: the answers have to be in a textbook, or on the blackboard, memorized for a test and then forgotten. Or they have to have seen it on television. They don't seem to develop logical-reasoning skills anymore. Reasoning seems to be dead."

Her husband nodded. On the trip they had stopped off at his brothers' homes in California and he'd spent several evenings with them. The big problem, as they saw it, was that they did not possess any unique accomplishments, something that might set them distinctly apart from other people around them. All three had begun to compare themselves with their deceased father, who had been active as a journalist, editor, and political personality. Their father had had a certain something, a personality of his own, special qualities they found lacking in themselves that had made him *him*. I tried to say that intergenerational comparisons lead nowhere, for world views change over time and what seems significant and important to one cohort may not impress the new cohorts in the same way: it may even seem irrelevant. Conversely, something that appeared incidental or insignificant to a past generation may take on unusual significance for a subsequent one. I connected this with my work on the death of meaning: with the decline of meaning, life itself can seem increasingly meaningless. In Hesse's words in *Steppenwolf*,[1]

A man of the Middle Ages would detest the whole mode of our present-day life as something far more than horrible, far more than barbarous. ... Now there are times when a whole generation is caught between two ages, two modes of life, with the consequences that it loses all power to understand itself and has no standard, no security, no simple acquiescence. Naturally, everyone does not feel this equally strongly. A nature such as Nietzsche's had to suffer our present ills more than a generation in advance. What he had to go through alone and misunderstood, thousands suffer today.

Without a panoply of meanings spread out above one, without the certainty of knowing what is the more desirable of two or more possibilities, the likelihood of seeing oneself in relations to others and the world becomes increasingly frustrating. The "other" becomes the one to blame. Frustration leads to aggression, and this aggression can take the form of complaints that the "other" has made one a "victim." One is always conscious of oneself as right and just and true and fair and honest: indeed, perhaps the last such one in the world. My mother used to tell a joke about a woman watching her son march in a post-World War I parade and proudly concludes, "Everyone is out of step but Jim."

This inability to admit one's own failings and to pass the blame to others was what my friend had noticed on his California trip. His brothers could find no clues to what was "wrong" with them, only that by their ages their father had made greater strides than they had. They vaguely suspected that opportunities for upward mobility had declined, rather than that they were found wanting, or that the world had changed and somehow had left them stranded.

The world had indeed changed, I suggested, and according to the data, traditional American upward mobility had declined with it. But there were still many productive people around and their presence needed explanation in light of his brothers' complaints, too. His wife agreed that the European and Asian students she taught were better students than the Americans and not as quick to blame others for their mistakes. Having noticed the same phenomenon, I asked her to explain it and she could not, other than noting that something had gone wrong in America, and we were just becoming aware of it. She related an example: she had to introduce some quantitative operations in her course material and was shocked to learn that her students had trouble not with such operations as calculus or even algebra, but with arithmetic itself. To her, a woman in her early thirties not long out of college, this was unimaginable. Arithmetic? Addition and subtraction, multiplication and division? What had happened?

Her husband returned to the tax problem. On their California trip the cashier at a restaurant told him the cash register wasn't working and she had to figure out the five-percent tax on a hand calculator. The tax, she said, came to one dollar. Since the bill was only ten dollars, he told her that was incorrect and that she should try again. She did and came up with the same answer. When he continued to object she called a fellow employee and asked her to check the tax calculation. She did so and came out with the same result. He tried to explain to them that a one-dollar tax on ten dollars service amounted to ten percent, not five percent, but they looked at him suspiciously, "How do you know that?" they asked, doubtful. He explained to them that ten dollars amounted to one thousand cents, and one tenth or ten percent of that was one hundred cents, or one dollar. And since five percent was half of ten percent then half of one hundred cents was fifty cents, and that was the tax. But it was clear that such notions as transitivity were beyond their comprehension; they stared at him dully, distrustful of his apparently glib attempt to "get something for nothing." Convinced that he was some kind of a "weirdo" or "nerd" and that further discussion with him might lead to an unpleasant scene, they took his fifty cents grimly and turned to the next customer on line, who simply paid what she was told.

These numbers my Wyoming friend was talking about clearly had no meaning for the waitress. The tax is something the cash register indicates as money due the government for a sale, and she saw no possibility of any computation she might make as legitimate in figuring taxes. Even hand calculators were not legitimate in this regard: they were used in classrooms, not in real life, and in real life the possibility of coming out with some number a customer objected to did not seem outlandish at all: customers always complained about prices and the level of service or the quality of the food. The possibility that there was anything in numbers themselves that dictated or determined the amount of tax, rather than simply the government's rules, never occurred to them.

Another example, drawn from the same California trip, but at another location:

He (customer): If I gave you a dollar for something costing forty-eight cents, how much change would I get?

She (sales cashier): I'll have to go to the cash register and see what the change is...

He: No, just figure it out.

She: How? My calculator...

He: Not by calculator, no.

She: Wait until I get a piece of paper, maybe I could do it that way ...

He: No, no, Can't you do it in your head?

She: In my HEAD?

He: Sure. If it cost fifty cents instead of forty-eight cents, how much change would I get?

She: I need a pencil and...

He: What is 50 to 100 as a fraction? 50 over 100?

She: How should I know?

He: Isn't fifty cents a half-a-dollar?

She: Yeah. So?

He: Well then?...

She: What's that got to do with it?

He: Forget it.

Listening to him recounting the incident I reminded him of Plato's *Meno* and the slave boy incident. We've come a long way in the past two thousand years, I mused. Yes, he said, a long way downward.

That many, if not most, people can no longer perform the simplest arithmetic operations "in their heads" is not the real problem here. The real problem is that they do not understand that numbers involve their own sets of meanings, and that these meanings may be applied to a near infinite variety of simple everyday events. The concept of a half applies not only to dollars but to all things that may be cut up or divided, to all wholes, that is. Again, meanings lie in relations between and among things, and this relationship is what constitutes what is called meaning in the first place. A half is a half of a whole, whatever the whole may be. The simplest sets of relations have become problems for everyday people as meanings fade away. The computer, the cash register, the calculator become the authorities, not the laws of numbers. That these devices are constructed about such laws but that the laws are not limited to them, but can be learned by ordinary people, does not seem to be evident to many.

Scholastic Aptitude Tests (SATs) measure a student's performance along two dimensions: the verbal and the quantitative. SAT scores have steadily declined for the past fifteen years, in spite of some random fluctuations at particular years. The trend is downward. Apologists try to claim it is because student populations are now more inclusive, drawn from many subcultural groups, while in the past it was largely white middle classes alone who were sampled by such tests. However, when ethnicity and economic class is controlled for statistically, the same results are obtained. White middle-class students' scores are dropping along with everyone else's, so the apology does not hold. Similar claims are made about intelligence quotient (IQ) scores: IQ tests are culturally specific, it is said, and, therefore, discriminate against minorities in the population who may not share the same cultural norms and socialization. This obscures the little significance such IQ scores have: they are measures of the probability of success in a predominantly white middle-class society. The apologists should argue that white middle-class society discriminates against nonwhites, not that the tests do. The tests only reflect the kinds of "intelligence" demanded to manipulate the life course in a predominantly white, middle-class, postindustrial society.

The decline of writing and computational ability makes itself felt in a number of ways. Even the front page of the highly respected *New York Times* frequently contains errors in spelling and sentence structure. I have not seen an issue in several years where such errors were absent. The kind of confusion this generates is compounded when the matter at hand is not the news, but information supposedly therapeutic or medicinal. I was recently shown a Seracult specimen envelope. Seracult is a procedure in which patients take their own stool samples and submit them through the mail to their physician's laboratory for evaluation. The instructions on the top of the envelope read as follows: "Do not use this envelope to mail specimens." Immediately below this, above a window, were the additional instructions: "You may put the return address for the slides on the mailing envelope through the window below." These instructions are entirely meaningless. Why would one include the return address (the laboratory's) on the mailing envelope if they did not include the specimen slides? The envelope is the only one included for the return of the slides and the patient is being cautioned to be certain the address shows, yet the instructions above tell the patient not to use the envelope for the slides! This is only one example of the inability to communicate that has resulted from the dilution of education and the decline of meaning.

A sociologist woman friend of mine, knowing of my interest in the death of meaning, recently recounted the following incident: She has been separated from her husband for more than two years and lives with her children in an apartment too small for them, a consequence of her husband's failure to provide the necessary child support. He has been contesting the divorce effort from its inception, and this has resulted in her running up thousands of dollars in legal fees. There is the usual bickering about visitations, who gets the care of the children and when, and similar pettiness associated with such divorce proceedings. When he does send money for child support, it is usually much less than expected in spite of his having an extremely high-salaried position with a major office and telecommunications company. Relations between them are bitter.

Recently, he sent her a greatly reduced check with a note that he was "strapped for cash" at the moment. He enclosed a zip-locked plastic bag containing some small onions, or shallots. "By the way," he said in the accompanying note, "here also are some shallots from my father's garden."

She stared at the plastic bag in disbelief. What could he possibly have had in mind in sending her these onions? They'd exchanged nothing but bitterness, hard words, and a few checks in the past few years, and now these onions? The onions were a meaningless gesture at best: she shared no meanings with him that would have included his offering her onions or shallots. He was not a gardener, a gourmet, or a short-order cook. He wrote speeches for executives, and she was a sociology professor. There was no common ground for a gratuitous offering of onions, and they were no substitute for the child support he was remiss in supplying. A humorless literalist, he could not have intended it as a bad joke. The incident was devoid of meaning.

Another respondent tells me of the trouble he experienced in cashing a check furnished him by his automobile insurance company. His vehicle was "totalled" in an accident over which he had no control: a driver without lights drove through a full-stop sign and smashed into his car, spinning it around several times. It was not a new car, and the total value recognized by the insurance company amounted to only $3500, not an inconsiderable sum, however, for a young man of limited income. When the insurance check arrived, he signed it and deposited it in his checking account. Later that month, after having written several checks against the account, he was startled to learn that his account was empty. He phoned the bank. "This is impossible," he told them." "I deposited a check for $3500 a few weeks ago and only wrote $200 in checks against it. Something is wrong." The bank could find no record of the deposit, whereupon he visited the bank in person and showed them the receipt he had obtained from the bank when he made the deposit. There was a certain amount of consternation on the part of the bank's management, but not nearly what he had expected. The bank promised to "look into it further," but after several weeks had not resolved the issue. Feeling like a character in a Kafka novel, the young man visited the bank again several times. It was clear he was not welcome and was viewed as an annoyance. Finally, the bank discovered a notation somewhere in their records that the check in question had only been signed by him, not co-signed by his insurance agent: both signatures were required, they told him. But, he replied, the teller who accepted the check and deposited it should have known that and told him so, precluding the deposit, and this was not done. Meanwhile, he was being denied the use of money rightfully his for several weeks. The bank finally admitted that they could find the check nowhere, and his receipt from them was the only evidence of its having existed. Desperate, he relayed his troubles to the insurance company, and the company agreed to cancel the original check and issue him a new one. He had the agent countersign it with him, and took it directly to the bank's officers, rather than to a teller, to cash it on the spot. While sitting at the desk of the junior assistant manager while the latter went behind a teller's window to return with the cash, he noticed a familiar-looking slip on the desk. Retrieving it, he found it to be the original "missing" check. The assistant manager, returning, was as surprised as he to find the check on his desk and mumbled something about "accidentally mislaying" it. My respondent left the bank in disgust.

What is most interesting about this incident is that it happened in a small suburban community rather than in a big city, and therefore illustrates the spread of meaninglessness beyond the metropolis where it is endemic. Slipshod operating procedures are not accidents: they are the consequences of failures in the operating system itself caused by the lack of understanding of the steps required in system maintenance. I had had a similar experience some twenty years earlier in moving from upstate New York to Manhattan. I withdrew $5000 from my account and had the bank write me a bank teller's check for that amount. Such a check is drawn against the bank, not the individual, and the funds are thus guaranteed. Across the street from the New School where I was joining the faculty was a branch of one of the largest banks in the nation, and I thought this a convenient place to open a checking account for my Manhattan tenure. The clerk at the desk was pleasant enough, eager to serve me, and the account was quickly opened, a number assigned to it by the computer, and my teller's check endorsed by me and handed over to the clerk. When the transaction was finished the clerk offered his hand for me to shake, and I accepted it. "One thing," I said, "I'll need some temporary checks to use until the printed ones arrive. Can you get me some?" I saw nothing unusual in this request, as I had followed this procedure everytime I'd moved in the past. But the clerk looked at me in amazement. "We have to wait until the check clears," he insisted. "Why?" I asked. "This is not my personal check, it's a bank teller's check, funds are guaranteed by the issuing bank." The clerk agreed. "But," he added, "we don't know who you are. The check might not be yours if you are not who you say you are."

"Look," I told him, "I'm a professor from across the street. If you want, come across the street with me and I'll introduce you to my dean, who will tell you who I am. You'll see my name on my office door, too, and I have the key to that. What more proof do you want?"

He shook his head. This made no difference, he insisted. That didn't prove I was the rightful owner of the check. This time I felt like a Kafka character. Why it made no difference was altogether incomprehensible to me. Either I was the person whose name was on the check or I was not, and I could prove that I was to anyone's satisfaction. This, however, did not seem to make any difference, because it did not fit the bank's operating procedures.

"Well then," I said, "give me back my check. There are plenty of banks in Manhattan anxious to have me as a client."

"We can't do that," he stated. "The sum has already been entered in the computer and the program does not allow us to withdraw it haphazardly like that."

Haphazardly? I began to make "a scene," as they say. I raised my voice so that it could be heard all over the bank and recounted to the world what had just transpired. A hurried conference was then conducted between a bank official and the clerk, who then smilingly informed me that the bank would let me have a few hundred dollars and would try to expedite the "check clearance process" on my behalf. Convinced that he was being magnanimous in his condecension to me, the bank official muttered something about the "stellar service to the community" being furnished by his organization, and I escaped quickly, determined to open another account elsewhere and let this one grow depleted.

I became convinced that when the money system becomes that disorganized in a city such as New York, within a mile of Wall Street, the center of American capitalism, something odd was happening to meanings.

If meanings are disappearing from American society, and meaning itself becoming a dead issue, it is not only in the area of cultural values and depleted vocabularies that this is evident. It is evident too in the most elementary operations, operations required to maintain a functioning society and a functioning economy: in computing change of currency, applying simple rules of proportion and percentage, and following policies that govern the most elementary banking operations.

After hearing my stories, my Wyoming friend mused that, like so many other things that are wrong with the present state of America, this seems to have originated in California and is spreading throughout the nation. "It's like the over-priced housing market," he offered, "or Disneyland. It's not only tasteless and pointless, it imposes a burden on everyone. Somehow it fits the picture of Ronald Reagan and Richard Nixon and George Bush: there is something corrupt at work here, something destructive. I'm not sure Bill Clinton is the answer to it." I agreed, but reminded him that it was only one of many such corruptions contributing to the meaningless anomic situation in American society. The people, typified by his brothers' complaints, were not the ones at fault, any more than the bank teller who failed to tell my respondent about the double signatures, the sales girls who could not figure out the difference between ten percent and five percent, or the bank clerk who could not understand how I could prove who I was by simply walking across the street. There was something external to them that was at fault, something in the larger society, something social. For perhaps the first time in history, the underpinnings of all relations had become wholly relativistic and arbitrary, and had lost the kind of absoluteness they had had in the past to make meaning secure and something to be shared.

As meaninglessness invades further areas of everyday life, what is signified by being a man, a woman, or a child in America is put up for grabs. Nothing is certain. Instead, the mere volitionless act of just *being*, just experiencing psychic stimuli unconnected with any semblance of meaning, becomes an everyday norm, a desirable end in itself, what one "ought" to do, and all other activity becomes pointless. It is as though the American population had taken too much LSD, too much acid back in the sixties, and was now tripping en masse. And there was no one outside of the trip to tell us what was happening to us, where we were or where we were going.

NOTE

1. Hermann Hesse, *Steppenwolf* (New York: Bantam), 1969, 24.

Chapter 10

Controlling Information

The inability of many high-school and college graduates to perform the simplest arithmetic operations without mechanical assistance points to an obvious flaw in their education. But their socialization may be at fault as well. The nationally syndicated family psychologist Dr. John Rosemund in his column "Parents and Kids" relates receiving a call from parents complaining that their six-year-old daughter was not doing well in school, and they were considering keeping her back so that learning would not be "frustrating for her" and she could then "enjoy school." The child was performing well but at an "average" level, although testing showed she had considerable "ability." Rosemund's comments on this are noteworthy:

These parents speak for many who seem to feel their job is to do whatever they can to buffer, if not altogether eliminate, frustration from their children's lives. Reality is this: Learning—true, meaningful learning—is always frustrating. The most valuable part of the experience, in fact, is learning that with effort one can overcome frustration; learning that, in the final analysis, it isn't how smart you are, but how determined. You don't learn this if your academic career is artificially engineered such that school is made easier and supposedly, more enjoyable. Such a strategy is, furthermore, likely to backfire, resulting not in an industrious child, but a lazy one.[1]

If "true, meaningful learning" is always frustrating, then it is clear that present day high-school and liberal arts college curricula that seek to make course material less frustrating and "easier" to master (in the process often depleting or eliminating the substantive content from the courses) deprive students of meaning. It is no wonder that my Wyoming friend encountered so many younger persons who could not perform the simplest arithmetic operations "in their heads." It is a frustrating operation at first, but decreases in its frustration as it is used redundantly and can become almost "second nature." Here the aggression resulting from frustration is focused on the problem, not upon others one seeks to blame. This was a traditional function of the socialization of the young in times of a "production-oriented" rather than "consumer-oriented" society. This later deprivation of such cultural skills is amplified by all "easy to learn" projects, television attempts only one among many. The most eloquent Public Television documentaries are poor substitutes for a well-written text on the subject. The decline of student skills and SAT scores correlates with the advent and popularity of the "learning is fun" approach of Sesame Street. Grade inflation is now demanded not only by parents, but by principals, deans, chancellors, and college presidents.

College textbooks these days mirror the junior-high textbooks of a generation ago: they are replete with pictures, often colored, with breezy language, and large type. Rather than being written by authorities in their respective fields, they are sometimes put together by committees of the publisher's editors, the designated author's name employed only as a legitimating device. They often come with "guides" for teachers, with ready-made quizzes and answers that make the teacher's understanding irrelevant to the meanings already determined by the editors. The vocabulary has been simplified so that no frustrating use of a dictionary is demanded of the student.

Concomitant with these efforts to eliminate concentration and grappling with the meaning of texts are planned political efforts to minimize or eliminate the flow and content of information to the public generally, not only to students. Information is increasingly controlled by government and the mass media have increasingly become henchmen of government. This was nowhere as evident as in the recent war between the United States and its allies with Iraq.

It is now estimated that more than 150,000 Iraqi soldiers and civilians were killed in "George Bush's war in the Persian Gulf," as it has come to be known.[2] We are told that only a few hundred British and American soldiers were killed. Such a slaughter ratio is abnormally high. I am no military historian, but I will hazard a guess that not since October 25, 1415, "Saint Crispin's Day," has there been such a fantastically high slaughter ratio in European history. One hundred English had died at the Battle of Agincourt that day. The French lost tens of thousands. At Agincourt there still remained some of that civility and honor among combatants that characterized the rules of medieval warfare. There were unarmed heralds such as Mountjoy of the French and Hereford of the English to watch and monitor the event, to see that the rules of medieval warfare were obeyed, to enforce a cease fire at the end of the day, to declare the day's winner and count the bodies: to serve as witnesses for the writing of the chronicles, the record books. In the Bush War in the Persian Gulf the nearest thing to heralds were the newspaper and TV cameramen, the chroniclers of the present day; but the Bush people barred them from the scene. They were not allowed to witness the carnage nor report it to the American public. In fact we know more about the Battle of Agincourt in 1415 than we know about the battles of Iraq or Kuwait. We know more about the D Day of World War II, Omaha Beach, Poussan, the Mekong Delta, the battles of Korea and Vietnam—all the American wars except those promulgated by George Bush in "the information age." In the Bush Wars the flow of information was tightly controlled. We are now, it was explained, an information society, so war must be fought with information as well as arms. The U.S. audience was shown nightly, on television, the skies over Baghdad, "the rockets' red glare, the bombs bursting in air," but no casualties, no blood and no wounded bodies, none of the body bags that were shown in the earlier wars. The world had changed, and American society with it. We have moved from an era of mechanism to an era of electronics. Grandfathers in the mechanical era had large round pocket watches that showed numerals arranged in a circle: such a watch showed present, past, and future hours and minutes on its face with its two hands. Today most grandfathers have watches that show only *Now* time, the present moment, in digital form: no past, no future extrapolations are possible on electronic digital wristwatches. The nature of the presentation of the present time, and that alone, is possible. A world that had gone from mechanism to electronics was the world presented in its latter form to the TV electronic audience: clean, neat, push-button precision. With information so controlled there was no way for the U.S. population to know what was in fact happening. Much has been written and said about the Bush War as a video-game war: push the button and zap pac man. The air of make-believe was exploited by Bush's generals and politicians. The U.S. viewer, hungry for news, was fed a diet of easily digested make-believe. Psychologists and sociologists discuss what is called "cognitive dissonance" and "cognitive inconsistency." In the Bush War the American audience experienced a national collective cognitive dissonance. In warfare, after all, there is death. There is blood, dismemberment. But in this war as it was electronically presented to them there was no death, no blood, no dismemberment. What the American audience expected to see was not ratified by their senses. The Bush War was thus a collective unreality, the negation of one's expectations—the opposite of what one knew must be happening or should be happening, and indeed could only be happening with the massive barrage of bombs raining down on Baghdad, night after night.

The euphoria, widespread through the United States at the end of the war and the return of the soldiers, was not so much a joy of winning the Bush War as a release from the collective cognitive dissonance experienced by the American TV audience. The world had returned: expectations could once again be ratified by ones senses. Society had not disappeared after all but was still there. This whole matter of cognitive dissonance or cognitive consistency had been explored by social psychologists (Leon Festinger, Fritz Heider, Osgood and Tannebaum) thirty years ago. There is a situation in Festinger's *When Prophecy Fails* where the true believers waited for the world to end, but it did not. They were left in a state of cognitive dissonance where their expectations were not ratified by their senses, and only when their prophetess guru rationalized God's blessing on them for their action and His decision not to end the world on their account did they experience that group euphoria shared by the American masses at the conclusion of the Bush War.[3] And for the same reason.

As plane load after plane load of local regiments landed, the local TV stations and newspapers bombarded their audiences with this proof of the past existence of the war (it must have happened, for where else were these people coming from?) and its redefinition of the Bush War as the new world order war: war is now not about body bags, dismemberment, death, blood and outrageous violence. War is now about clean-cut young men and women stepping off airplanes into the arms of cheering fathers, mothers, lovers, wives, husbands, the new order in the American family reflected in the nonviolent battlefield on the sand dunes of Saudi Arabia. The Bush War reflects the new American preoccupation with fun (Is it a fun thing? Can't classes be made fun? Can't war be fun? Was the Bush War a *fun* thing?). The collective euphoria was universal. It was as if the United States had fought a war and nobody even got hurt. There was a saying among the youth culture of the 1960s in the United States: "Some day they'll hold a war and nobody will come." But this time everybody came, and it was a fun thing, a TV event for everyone except the dead Iraqis. It was especially so for the emir of Kuwait and his family, who sat it out in the air-conditioned casinos of Monte Carlo, throwing dice and buying women. As a soap opera it made top TV ratings, even surpassing the "Who Shot J. R. Ewing? " of *Dallas*.

Some commentators have claimed that the enthusiasm of the American people for the Bush War was a result of their collective guilt at losing the war in Vietnam and shunning the returning soldiers. They had failed to drag out the brass bands and the yellow ribbons and the flags for the losers. Later, in remorse, Americans erected the monument in Washington, D.C. that characterizes that war, a black scar at the heart of the nation, the names of its dead chiseled into the scar's surface. It was a growing appreciation for those who sacrificed in Vietnam that prompted the Americans to tie yellow ribbons on trees and display flags and patriotic banners and "support the boys at the front in Saudi Arabia." But there is little to support such a view. Up until the very moment that Bush unleashed his first bombardment of Baghdad, every major religious group in the United States had insisted that war was not the solution, that negotiation was demanded. And negotiation was offered by Saddam Hussein but rejected by Bush, who insisted that there was no point in talking and who, therefore, demanded an unconditional surrender. Bush, like Hitler unleashing his blitzkrieg on Spain, was eager to test out his new weapons. As the Spanish Civil War had its Guernica, so the Bush War had its Baghdad. A push-button war had been on the books since the end of World War II because of the Soviet-U.S. rivalry. The president and his top military officers carried about with them, wherever they roamed, "a push button in a box" that could start a nuclear war. But with the collapse of the Soviet empire the push-button box became an anachronism. Nevertheless, so much had been invested in "smart weaponry" that a real test was demanded and consequently furnished by the renegade of the CIA in the Persian Gulf.

The earlier Bush War, in Panama, had not presented such an opportunity. There were of course similarities—Noriega, like Hussein, had been a paid U.S. henchman until he "went bad and struck out on his own" and, therefore, had to be punished. The Bush rhetoric was identical. Bush compared Hussein to Hitler, as he had Noriega. And the American people were not allowed to see what happened in Panama, either. Indeed, this petty bush league war (it only killed a few thousand Panamanians) was a kind of dry-run test for the Iraqi Bush War. There were some differences, of course. The Bushites captured Noriega at last and put him in jail where he languished without a trial, much like Richard II. Saddam Hussein, however, was allowed to go free as soon as the Kuwaiti oil wells were liberated. The TV heralds were allowed to show the blasted tanks, trucks, cars, half tracks, and jeeps destroyed by the allies as the Iraqis fled north; but no bodies, no dead Iraqis. The media was allowed to show only *violence against things*, not *violence against persons*. The Bush War was thus portrayed in its iconographic discourse as a less barbaric enterprise than, let us say, the Battle of Agincourt of 1415. This was a triumph of iconography over the past denotative meanings inherent in words. It is symptomatic of what happens when word-derived meanings are destroyed and carefully selected pictures are substituted in their place. Showmanship, iconography, and media manipulation reached its highest point on May 5, 1991, when the U.S. government hired the Walt Disney Company to stage a gigantic Hollywood-style spectacle in Tampa, Florida, for welcoming home the commanding general of the allied forces, General Shwartzkopf.

What, then, is to be learned from the images and graphic displays of the Bush wars? From the standpoint of an invading army, such as the American-European allies, it would seem at first devoid of meaning. It was the Nazis, after all, who practiced saturation bombing by the Luftwaffe before the Panzer divisions were sent in, followed by the troops to mop up. The allies did the same thing in the Bush War: control the skies first and then you can control the ground. World War II ended and these same allies learned from the Germans and eliminated the Iraqi air force first. And Baghdad was bombed as Berlin had been bombed, unrelentingly, night after night to break the will of the civilian population.

There is not much to be learned from this employment of now-traditional modes of modern warfare. There were, however, certain public relations innovations and the use of political power on the home front that must be recognized. The perhaps inadvertent creation of a collective cognitive dissonance about the actual warfare and the resulting release or removal of that dissonance for the creation of a national euphoria is a political maneuver that, once it is pointed out, will probably be used with increased frequency by political structures the world over. Another point: personifying the enemy is not new: the "Jap" or the "Hun" as stereotypes of one's enemies is an old device. But it must be remembered that in World War II (for example) the allies did not make Adolf Hitler the personified enemy: there were Goebbels and Goering, Himmler and Hitler; mostly it was "the Nazis" and "the Japs." And in Korea and Vietnam it was "communism." But in both Bush Wars, in Panama and in Iraq, it was the head of state, Noriega and Hussein, who were personified by the political administration as the enemy. These are concrete images, unlike the hazy "communism" and "Nazism." These images helped contribute to the dissonance, for although they were targeted as "the enemy," the actual portrayal of the warfare furnished by the authorities paid little attention to them once hostilities were underway. Once victory was at hand, there was some speculation about the location of Hussein but no effort to capture him. With Panama, focus was once again placed on Noriega, hiding out in the Vatican's embassy. The U.S. command saw fit to employ the most tasteless rock-and-roll music to bombard his sanctuary and drive him to surrender. An adult can tolerate hard rock-and-roll music at teenage intensities only so long, and Noriega was no exception. So the Panama affair offered a unique form of warfare that resulted in surrender.

Encouraging mass support for the troops, rather than the war itself or the possible goals of the warfare, was employed on TV and through other media by the Bushites to distract attention from the barbarity of the slaughter. Americans were encouraged by their government and the media to tie yellow ribbons around trees, fly flags, proclaim their support loudly for the troops. At no time whatever did the government encourage support of the war. This was probably due to the earlier expression of opposition by the churches and the saner members of the political establishment. Black Americans in particular kept up vigorous opposition to the war. Students demonstrated, but the media, anxious to retain favor with the administration, shielded the public from such images and showed pictures of demonstrations to "support the troops." And when the war ended, the media followed through with shots of groups "supporting the troops" as they disembarked from their planes.

If we set these things in order, we can see how the control of information was maneuvered to project a particular meaning at odds with the manifest meaning of what at best was a nonlegitimate military enterprise. The steps followed are these:

1. Equating the enemy with the image of the head of state and implying that although he was an ally in the past, he has gone bad and betrayed us. This calls forth a wholly emotive response. It is Judas and his like we envision.

2. Shifting the focus of images from warfare to support of the troops. This was made a troop phenomenon but there was the certainty that sufficient superiority was at hand so that the number of troops killed

could be reported as few. No mention was made of the casualties of the enemy, particularly of the most defenseless civilians, women, children, and the elderly.

3. Barring the press from participation. The press was not allowed to accompany the troops as in the past. This resulted in complete control of the flow of information, and the press was grateful for whatever scraps of information, or misinformation, was given them. There were none of the Ernie Pyles of World War II.

4. Editing visual information furnished to the press. Precautions were taken so that the press showed violence against *things*, not against *people* to the American viewer.

5. Focusing on the troops, rather than the warfare. It was relatively easy to highlight pictures of the victorious troops returning home and to maintain the illusion of a nonviolent war. The event became a troop movement phenomenon, rather than an exercise in violence.

6. The use of overwhelming force against a smaller, weaker enemy. An enemy who did not share the same cultural background in the development of its technological weaponry.

We can expect these six steps to be followed by other nations or even by the United States in the future. The likelihood of cognitive disorientation on the home front will thus be optimized and the political institution receive overwhelming support.

This may seem Machiavellian, but Machiavellianism is an ideology that has not been foreign to Western political institutions. Machiavelli wrote *The Prince* in 1513, ninety-eight years after the slaughter of the French by the English at Agincourt. His model prince was Cesare Borgia, the illegitimate son of the corrupt pope, Alexander VI, at a time when Spain ruled most of Italy and the Spanish families, such as the Borgias, represented unbridled political and military ambition. Borgia was Machiavelli's "Prince of Foxes," whose main purpose was to rule as a prince by cunning and manipulation. Machiavelli was himself a republican, however, not a royalist, and the extent to which he had his tongue in his cheek when he described the ruthless procedures necessary to maintain power has long been a subject of debate. We must not mistake George Bush for a Prince of Foxes, however; he had neither the wit nor the sophistication of a Cesare Borgia or a Machiavel. But he had Machiavellians about him as advisors. And they did remarkably well in creating and managing the Bush Wars.

The Battle of Agincourt, in 1415, was fought on the Anglican holy day, St. Crispin's day, and the ratio of slaughter exceeded or at least equaled the ratio in the Bush War. The English forces had consisted of only 9,000 men-at-arms when they first landed at Calais. But the arduous march and the ravages of disease plagued the army, and Henry V turned about to head back toward the coast when he had lost some 2,000 men to hunger, disease and plague. His rag-tag army met the waiting French, the smug princes of Armagnac and Burgundy and their well-armed hosts. The men-at-arms and the knights of both sides were equipped with the latest technology of the time, including the use of bombards with gunpowder. Both sides wore elegant armor, fashioned by the finest Italian armorers of the strongest steel, covered with the multicolored fabric jupons bearing their heraldic crests, the golden lions of England and the fleur-de-lis of France.

The way Shakespeare tells it, 184 years later, with all the exaggeration of the ethnocentric Englishman, the French lost ten thousand men, only fifteen hundred of whom were hired mercenaries, "The rest are princes, Barons, Lords, Knights, squires, and gentlemen of blood and quality" and their names are given. The English, he tells us, lost four noblemen and twenty-five men at arms. And he has his good King Harry, Henry the Fifth, tell his victorious knights,

> This story shall the good man teach his son:
> And Crispin Crispian shall neer go by,
> From this day to the ending of the world,
> But we in it shall be remembered . . .
> He that outlives this day and live old age,
> Will yearly on the vigil feast his neighbors
> And say, *Tomorrow is Saint Crispin's Day*;
> Then will he strip his sleeve and show his scars,
> And say, *These wounds I had on Crispin's Day.*
> . . . And gentlemen of England now a-bed,
> Shall think themselves accursed they were not here;

And hold their manhoods cheap whilst any speaks
That fought with us upon St. Crispin's Day.

Henry V, IV, 3

And there is a certain truth in that; we still remember Harry and his little band of Englishmen, striving to re-take their continental homeland, Normandy, land of their fathers, back from the French and return it to the legitimate heirs, the Norman descendants of William the Conqueror, the Plantagenet kings of England. It is doubtful, of course, whether George Bush will be remembered for the Bush Wars, as King Harry is remembered for Agincourt. Despite the similar slaughter ratios, the Bush Wars, unlike Agincourt, were not combat between two nations sharing a common technological culture and similar resources. The straggling English force that landed at Normandy in 1415 can not be likened to the massive buildup in Saudi Arabia in 1990, conducted over months in friendly territory, of the American-European allies.

St. Crispin's Day has been honored for centuries in Britain. But there is no "Day" on which to honor the Bush War in Arabia, or his earlier war in Panama. Who remembers the date of the day only a few years ago, on which the Bush War in Arabia was supposed to have ended? What veteran will strip his sleeve and say he was there, in Arabia, when the enemy never appeared and the war that was bloodless and victimless was won by the transistors and the diodes, the smart bombs and the semiconductors, the information brokers and the public-relations promoters? What he will remember is the going, and most of all, the homecoming, the ribbons and the flags, the crowds at the airport—discovering that he was a hero for just having been there, away from home on an unplanned vacation. It was hot, and dry, and there was all that sand, he will say. But the food wasn't too bad, considering.

If we understand violence itself as a discourse, a way of presenting data about selected things, then the discourse on violence has changed over the centuries. It is clear that back in 1415, the discourse on violence in warfare primarily concerned itself with violence against human bodies and was conveyed in words. The greatest of English writers tells us that the Agincourt veteran was to roll up his sleeve and display his scars, and Shakespeare gives us an extended, if incorrect, count of the number of bodies, French and English, found upon the field. Not so in 1991. Neither the American-European command nor the Iraqi command told us anything about bodies; body counts, particularly with respect to the Iraqis, has had to be inferred by independent, dissenting agencies. What was emphasized by both the American-European and the Iraqis were images of the damage done to the so-called "infra-structure"—the number of bridges destroyed, tanks put out of action, command posts bombarded, water supply, and electrical power facilities struck out of commission and oil wells set on fire. So this discourse on violence now concerns *things*, not *people*. Michel Foucault found something similar with respect to judicial punishment and imprisonment in the West, and with respect to sexuality and a number of other discursive phenomena. Something similar has been occurring respecting warfare.

But something else has occurred with respect to warfare as well. In celebrating the slaughter of the French in 1415, the English, including Shakespeare, reiterate its association with Saint Crispin's Day, thus lending an air of religious awe and respect, of holiness, to the endeavor. The English knights carried into battle, after all, certain icons: the cross of Saint George, the red cross on a white background. The French bore the red banner, the Oriflamme, symbol of the Christian passion, and the chronicles mention these repeatedly. But the Bush War, for all its enlarged TV iconography, was not so celebrated, or associated with religious icons or values. The churches had, after all, opposed the war until it was no longer possible to do so. Bush went ahead and bombed Baghdad despite them, and once this was done, the churches meekly submitted. Thus, transcendental values were absent in the rhetoric of the Bush War, while present at Agincourt. Transcendental values, after all, are idealized sets of meanings, and, therefore, can be expected to be among the first to suffer as meaning itself disappears.

The ways of waging wars have changed, but so have the ways of delineating war. By controlling information and substituting images for verbal facts, feelings for meanings, and by employing videographic advances not only for the direction of missiles but for the direction of public sentiments, a new and dangerous level of warfare has begun. As in so many social phenomena we have examined in these chapters, the iconographic has replaced the meaningful demotic, and the meanings hitherto associated with such things as warfare and destruction rendered more uncertain by their newly acquired lack of meaning.

NOTES

1. John Rosemund. "A Determined Effort to Learn Can Overcome Frustration." Syracuse *Post Standard*, July 16, 1992.

2. Much of the following material is drawn from my invited lecture to the Society For Strategic Studies, Republic of China, Taipei, Taiwan, on May 21, 1991.

3. Leon Festinger, H. W. Riecken, and S. Schachter, *When Prophecy Fails*, (Minneapolis: University of Minnesota Press), 1956.

Chapter 11 _____

The Competition for Definitions

In the previous chapters I have discussed some of the various forces at work that, intentionally or inadvertently, promote the destruction of meaning. Some are governmental efforts to extend its authority or control its population, as in the use of images by political parties or the administration in the Bush wars. Some are fostered by purely economic concerns, as efforts to gain a more complete control over the buying habits of the individual by ridding the individual of all social bonds and hence promote consumerism. Others come about in a circular fashion, for as meanings die and individuals are left stranded in a world of pointless existence, they seek desperately to explain their unexpected isolation and frustration by blaming others and seeking more power for themselves, further depleting the possibility of a meaningful existence.

Meanings change, and always have; that is to be expected as the life worlds of successive generations change. In addition, there has always been some competition among groups to dominate definitions of situations. Early in this century the American sociologist W. I. Thomas of the University of Chicago pointed to this rivalry, and later Robert K. Merton wrote his now-famous essay employing Thomas's "definition of the situation." Situations perceived as real are real in their consequences. The "Last

National Bank," as Merton called it in his example, failed because a rumor had started that the bank was failing, causing a run on the bank that finally, indeed, did cause the bank to fail. It would not have failed otherwise. Thus, he argued, collectivities of people may cause some social events to happen inadvertently. People do indeed make the world they live in, but they do so with a great deal of inadvertence and lack of intentionality. Thus was born the famous "self-fulfilling prophecy" of sociological fame.

But it is not the simple historical change in meanings that is so evident at the close of this century: it is the diminution of meaning itself. Thomas was concerned with the definition of situations because at the turn of the century different people defined situations differently. Later insights, from Michel Foucault and others, showed the connection that often exists between the desire for power and such discursive attempts at redefinitions. Depending upon the power capabilities of the group, it may impose its definition of the situation upon others by various means: coercion, fear, terror, propaganda, education, through the courts, governmental acts, and the like. Groups develop around ideologies, and ideologies cement groups into communities, particularly in historical situations where community, in the sense of the ancient polis, is seriously absent but the need to belong is not. Ideologies are attempts to impose definitions favorable to the group or camp espousing them. Once such definitions are imposed they need not convince anyone of their "truth" or "reliability." They have consequences by virtue of their mere expression and latent appeal to the frustrated individual. Indeed, only the "true believers" believe these definitions are "true" and are taken for granted. Other groups continue to hold to their own ideologies, however culturally derived, and still contend with the dominant group that has imposed its definitions through the courts or otherwise. Traditionally this was most true of religious beliefs (which are ideologies of a certain kind), but in recent years, as religious complexions have changed, it has been extended by partisan activists to almost every field of activity. The nationwide growth of popular culture and the persuasiveness of the media have made it possible for any group to make its claim that it has been victimized and, therefore, must be heeded. These seek to make their claim to legitimacy by misapplying key concepts that were originally used in quite different contexts and, therefore, involved different meanings than the ones they seek to impose. In democratic states such key words as *equality, freedom, justice* are employed because of the emotive appeal these words acquired in earlier usages. In the United States, for example, equality originally meant political equality— the right to vote—freedom meant freedom from England, and justice meant that the laws were applied equally to each *person*. In the later quest for power over others sought by competing ideological groups, however, equality came to signify social sameness, freedom came to mean independence of any social constraints, and justice came to mean that the laws were applied disproportionately to members of specific groups, as in Affirmative Action programs.

In place of the collective conscience, a kind of "group mind" defined earlier by Durkheim, contemporary societies are often characterized by fierce competition between and among these different ideological groups, each seeking to dominate definitions of situations in ways to make them most favorable to themselves.

The raping of rape is an example of this. Largely through the complaints of radical feminists, for example, some states have adopted a definition of rape espoused and promoted to satisfy feminist power demands. The media, as we have seen, play a large part in attempting to legitimate these efforts. The media are servants of the economy and cannot risk, they believe, any position that might offend a substantial part of their market. Indeed, the continual decline in media quality, most noticeable in television programming, has resulted from the market demands perceived by the TV broadcast industry. Programs are continued or cancelled depending, not upon their quality, but the mere numbers of viewers tuned in to them. Thus, TV fare continually sinks to the lowest common denominator and results in infantile situation comedies having no resemblance to the life worlds of its viewers and devoid of any intellectual content whatever. Commercial TV cannot have meanings, nor can it deal with meanings; it seeks the salacious, the sensational, the titillating, not the true or the real, the enlightening or the transcendant. It makes its appeal to the hormones and the glands, not to the heart and the brain, in Faulkner's sense. It does this not only in its ongoing attempts at "entertainment" in the increasingly lurid soap operas, for example, but even in more serious pseudo-news coverage, such as the Anita Hill affair, or innumerable murder trials. Chained to that which has no meaning, therefore, TV and the related media accelerate the decline and death of meaning itself. The function of TV and the press has become one of entertainment and diversion, not of enlightenment. It is difficult to believe that the framers of the Constitution had the entertainment industry in mind when they guaranteed the freedom of the press, but that is what has occurred: news is presented as entertainment, not as significant current events. This was as true in the Bush Wars as in all other events reported upon. Even serious occurrences are treated as mere sensation and manipulated to excite the audience. The excitement is always brief, however, and more "news" must be instantly invented to stir the jaded appetites of a public seeking "fun" and thrills in the abandonment of serious discourse encouraged by its institutions.

The decline in newspapers correlates with the rise of television news. But TV news items are 30- or 60-second bites that consider each and every event as equal to each and every other event; the only salience of an "item" is the order in which it is scheduled to appear on the regular six P.M. and eleven P.M. news programs. Enough items must be secured to fill these time slots, and each is chipped away to maximum emotion and minimal duration. A riot, an earthquake, an election in France, internal strife in Yugoslavia, or the assassination of a head of government are all treated as equal events and afforded equal coverage with the winner of the soap-box derby or the latest divorce gossip from Hollywood. Thus, the relative significance of any event is lost. Differences among events become unimportant. The meaning of any event, if it is not connected with instant gratification or "fun," is accordingly destroyed. "Human interest" stories have increasingly displaced news items, making the news broadcast more of a magazine than a newspaper. The human interest story, carefully selected, tends to cater to the salacious rather than the informative. In addition, the time slot is increasingly filled with nonnews items: the latest in diet fads, health regimens, medical techniques, child-rearing practices.

Ferdinand de Saussure and the later structuralists were able to show that it is the relation among words and things, not the words and things themselves, which embody and convey meaning.[1] The set of words in the sentence "John hits the ball" is identical to that in "The ball hits John" but the meaning is quite different because the relations of the words to one another is different. In our cognition it is these sets of relations among things that enable us to perceive what we call meaning. From this perspective, therefore, we might expect that as relations among persons declined, meanings would decline as a consequence, and that as meanings declined, relations among persons would decline as well. Claude Levi-Strauss, Mauss's successor to the chair of cultural anthropology at the College of France, argued (not always convincingly) that the language system was the social system *par excellence* and that all other social systems emulated or copied it, so that the organization of a village could be read as a sentence, for example.[2] However this may be, and certainly not all anthropologists agree, the thesis that meanings lie in the relations between and among words or between and among things has not, until now, been properly juxtaposed to the Durkheim and Mauss primitive classification thesis:[3] the relations among people cognitively determines the relations among things. For if indeed this is true, that the classification of things follows the classification of men, and if indeed meaning—and therefore classification—lies in relations and not in the things themselves or the words themselves, then a symbiotic situation exists in which as relations between individuals become more tenuous, meanings become more tenuous, and as meanings become more tenuous, relations between persons becomes more tenuous: we become trapped in an ever-increasing uncertainty where meaning itself becomes a victim, as we ourselves become victims. That is the central conclusion of the present study. It becomes quite clear that persons have increasing difficulty in relating to other persons in the absence of agreed-upon meanings. A "meaningful relationship" becomes unthinkable where meanings are no longer available to mediate the connections, the social bonds, between and among individuals. The emergence of the monad at the close of the century, this unattached individual lacking not only community but indeed connection to any other human being in family, in marriage, in social organization of any kind—the "single parent," the "unwed mother," the earphoned jogger, or walk-manned student bobbing his or her head with raucous musical noise to preclude any inner reflectiveness or contemplation that might challenge the inability to connect to another—has resulted in little more than sexual exploitation between individuals of opposite or same sexual "preferences." The increase in teenage alcoholism, teenage pregnancies, and teenage violence exploited by the sensationalist press are only what we might expect in a society where the young are not socialized in acceptable social behavior or in intellectuality, where grades are inflated and social deviance not only tolerated but encouraged by indulgent parents, the press, and the ever-growing popular culture industry. This industry, like all marketplace enterprises, now profits from destroying bonds between individuals and rendering them anomic monads, eager to snatch whatever commodities are offered in their desperate attempts at a "selfhood" no longer possible.

In the new American society developing at the close of the twentieth century there is an abundance of these unattached monads, but such unattached monads cannot constitute a society: societies are constituted by social bonding among individuals. Social institutions exist to encourage such bonding: in the family, the body politic, education, and in the religious belief in something greater than the now-disappearing self. The web of social affiliations makes society possible, not a war of all against all. So the new American society cannot be a society if it is populated exclusively by such monads. Fortunately, at this late date some dyadic marriages and triadic families are still forming in the face of highly deterministic pressures from without, resisting the monadic, atomistic pressures promulgated by the media, the market, and juvenile popular culture. But the face of things has changed and will change further as meaning dies and the enterprise appears more problematic and less satisfying.

NOTES

1. Ferdinand de Saussure, *Course in General Linguistics* (New York: McGraw-Hill), 1959.

2. Claude Levi-Strauss, *Structural Anthropology* (New York: Basic Books), 1963.

3. Emile Durkheim and Marcel Mauss, *Primitive Classification* (Chicago: University of Chicago Press), 1963.

Chapter 12

The Death of Oedipus

The death of meaning has had other unanticipated consequences. The efflorescence of aggressive behaviors on an unprecedented scale is one consequence of the frustration
experienced by an increasing number of unattached individuals.
Unable to make any social bonds to others, even to their parents,
the emerging individuals, male and female, find themselves in
a pointless, normless milieu where destructive impulses are
vented against unsuspecting bystanders. The Los Angeles riots
following the Rodney King verdict is only one example of a
phenomenon that occurs at a less advertised level throughout
the nation. One can no longer predict what will trigger an av-
alanche of destruction and hatred. Frustration is no longer a cue
for looking inward, for determining the internal failures that
have led to the inability to cope with the complexities of the
world, to explain one's own failings and seek to correct them.
Instead, frustrated monads vent their aggression on others while
blaming these same others for their victimization. Sometimes
this takes sexual forms, sometimes political or economic exploitation is involved. Cadres of self-appointed "victims" arise to
vigorously challenge all others, and a society of differentiated
victims of an infinite variety is created to tear away at any alter-
nate claim to legitimacy but their own. Meeting the opposition

of similarly self-defined cadres, they find themselves unable to enforce their demands and their frustration level rises to the ignition point. This is clearly what occurred on a grand scale April 19, 1993 on the part of the FBI and the Texas Rangers, who, after a long siege, were unable to enforce their demands on a commune of Christian fundamentalists preparing for a "war of the Saints against the worldly Beast of the Apocalypse." The frustrated FBI agents and Texas Rangers then violently assaulted the armed Christian stronghold near Waco, Texas, killing some 87 men, women and children in a blazing inferno.

In the first half of the century Freudian explanations abounded for the less frequent occurrences of such aggression. But the usual Freudian explanations have ceased to be satisfactory since the new narcissistic monads do not conform to those well-established patterns of abnormal behaviors hitherto considered neurotic. The monad is a new aberrant personality type, and other than traditional explanations must be employed to understand his or her destructive behavior. It is not unexpected, therefore, that the oft-cited Oedipal explanations are heard far less frequently these days than they were in our parents' and grandparents' days.

Although the fictional Oedipus died several thousand years ago, he was resurrected early in this century by the efforts of Sigmund Freud and Freud's reification of a literary theme into a "universal complex." Oedipus then quickly became the most celebrated mythical character in American cocktail party culture. But explanations of the early popularity of Oedipus in the United States are not particularly satisfying since they always omit the unique historical conditions necessary to make such a reification possible. The psychologistic nature of popular culture in the first half of this century predisposed the population to the introduction of a vocabulary rich in sexual imagery and allusion in its effort to repudiate the supposedly repressive Victorian discourse of its immediate past: *supposedly* because, as Michel Foucault has shown, our insistence that sexual repression was and is everpresent is suspicious and likely inaccurate in its various implications.[1] By escaping the causal responsibility for one's actions (which is what the Oedipus story is really about) and seeking to explain human actions in terms of the laws of causality implicit in the natural sciences, Freudian explanation opened the door to a repudiation of the rational Aristotelian idea that human action originated in the actor himself and the actor was, therefore, wholly responsible for his actions. Such a rational explanation of human action characterized the idea of responsibility enunciated by the French school of social thought at the time.[2] The Freudian explanation set this aside and in doing so became immediately popular. Assigning the blame for one's misdeeds on someone or something external to one's own self, and, therefore, over which one had no personal control, was welcomed as the most liberating notion ever promulgated in the name of science.

In the first half of this century the monadic individual had scarcely begun to emerge; instead, marriage rates and family sizes were beginning to increase, and stable SAT scores and continual upward mobility were taken for granted as indicators of sound national health. The Freudian intrusion was therefore the first sign that despite this, something was going amiss; "free will" and self-determination, although strongly embedded concepts in the American conscience, were starting to waver. The transition from newsprint to icons had just begun with the advent of the motion picture and accelerated with new glossy picture magazines like *Life* and *Look*; by the 1950s television was only beginning to make its entrance into the home. Progressive education of the John Dewey variety had been introduced into more and more schools from the 1930s on. "Emotional adjustment" of students, rather than intellectual accomplishment, was beginning to be pushed by educators on a national basis. Some social critics sensed that something was changing, something untoward was happening. David Riesman sensed it in his *Lonely Crowd* of 1950 and tried to connect it with changing demographics and the replacement in the population of inner-directed persons by "other directedness" based not upon any internalized moral standards, but on observations of what others were doing.[3] Later, in the second half of the century, when the Freudian sedimentation had become thoroughly entrenched and the monadic personality had fully emerged, Christopher Lasch, in *Culture of Narcissism*, would see beyond Riesman's lonely crowd to the emerging narcissism focused on the self and an omnipresent

Now.[4] But in the first half of the century the narcissistic direction was scarcely observed, and it was Oedipus who emerged as the primary subject of cocktail chit-chat and literary criticism, the darling of the self-proclaimed "sexually liberated" intelligentsia in Boston, New York, and Chicago.

The stage was set in the first decades of this century for a language appropriate to our "other directed" sexual attractions, and Freud strode upon the stage and retold the Athenian drama to audiences who otherwise might not have heard of this mythical, one time King of Thebes but would have been satisfied with the newly pictured exploits of Rin Tin Tin and Little Orphan Annie.

Freud at that time also spoke of an "Electra complex," a kind of female analog or equivalent of the male Oedipus complex. Because of the double standard in American culture at the time (women were still "pure" and men were "oversexed") the Electra complex had less appeal than its complement, and as the end of the century approached, it has been vigorously denounced along with penis envy and related negative images of womanly wants. However, the eagerness with which Oedipus was embraced and Electra dismissed now appears more significant than it appeared at the time. Electra was the daughter not of King Oedipus of Thebes but of King Agamemnon of Argos, to whom her libido was so strongly affixed that she conspired to convince her brother Orestes to murder their mother, whom she hated with a vengeance. Eugene O'Neill fashioned an American version in his trilogy, *Mourning Becomes Electra*, transposing the story from Argos and the war with Troy to the American South and the Civil War.

Why had Oedipus dominated the cocktail party chatter of the earlier period and not Electra? We might conjecture that in the newly liberated sexual banter of the time, the fact that Oedipus had indeed slept with his mother and fathered four children with her in the process, while Electra had only fantasized sleeping with her father, may have made Oedipus the more titillating subject. Electra had not produced offspring for her father; and after all, even if she had, there was precedent for daughters doing that in some of the Bible stories of the ancient patriarchs. At the time, too, American women were relatively overprotected and American culture could not then have characterized itself in any matter in terms of the female sex, and probably still cannot despite the political posturing now evident. The Statue of Liberty may stand in New York Harbor, but to most Americans she is peculiarly French. The United States is still a fatherland, not a motherland, and the rejection of motherhood in contemporary discourses guarantees that it will remain so for a while.

If, in the first three quarters of this century, we saw Oedipus everywhere (Ernest Jones saw him not only in *Hamlet*, as did Laurence Olivier, but in Joyce's Stephen Daedalus and else-where), today Oedipus seems curiously absent. He may be so taken-for-granted that he manages to escape our conversation. Something has happened to Oedipus in American society. In the newly emerging puritanism he has become old hat, passé, out of date, trite. We would be embarrassed to bring up his name at a cocktail party today, unlike the situation fifty years ago when he was all the rage. Today we limit his name to the classroom, where it is relatively certain that no one will remember who he was beyond the scheduled quiz for that part of the course. Why is this? Has our sexually-oriented discourse become less signif-icant? Foucault's work tends to cast doubt on such an assumption. Has the heralded "decline of the family" made the House of Laius less interesting? Do we assume now that since, after all, Oedipus did not really know Jocasta was his mother he did not experience any forbidden thrill in consorting with her, so there was nothing salacious in the story to begin with and only its Victorian antithesis made it fascinating to earlier Americans? That there was nothing sinful about it after all, or, perhaps, since the meaning and use of the word *sin* is in decline, that every woman is fair game for every man and vice versa whatever the social or "family relation"? Or, because of the sudden interest in older women sleeping with younger men, that Jocasta was a kind of liberated pioneer in this area? Is even the meaning of *incest* vanishing? Whatever the reason (and for all the facetious manner above I do think that all of these reasons apply) Oedipus finally is dead. He may have died at Colonos a few thousand years ago, but to our liberated and increasingly meaningless discourse on sexuality he died again only recently. It has been a while since I have heard anyone blame someone being overweight on that man's Oedipal cravings, or Junior's aggression on his attempt to exorcise his Oedipal.

It is interesting that social critics, commentators, and psychiatrists seem to be saying much the same thing, although in other ways, since they come to their conclusions from discourses other than the sociological. According to psychiatrist Joel Kovel.

The stimulation of infantile cravings by advertising, the usurpation of parental authority by the media and the schools, and the rationalization of inner life accompanied by the false promise of personal fulfillment, have created a new type of "social individual." . . . The result is not the classical neurosis where an infantile impulse is suppressed by patriarchal authority, but a modern version in which impulse is stimulated, perverted and given neither an adequate object upon which to satisfy itself nor coherent form of control. . . . The entire Complex, played out in the setting of alienation rather than direct control, loses its classical form of symptom.[5]

It is this "new type of social individual" that has come on stage to replace the deceased Oedipus now that meaninglessness is becoming the norm. Richard Sennett reminds us,

The hysterical symptoms which were the dominant complaints of Freud's erotic and repressive society have largely disappeared. This character disorder has arisen because a new kind of society encourages the growth of its psychic components and erases a sense of meaningful social encounter outside its terms, outside the boundaries of the single self, in public.[6]

Both Sennett and Lasch are pointing to the monadic individual immersed in the meaningless environment we have been discussing. Lasch saw the emerging American culture as a culture of narcissism. But although the monadic society is characterized by such narcissists, the term is misleading since it conjures up the myth of the beautiful young man of classical legend: Narcissis. Narcissis, however, was involved in "primary narcissism" according to Lasch, not the "secondary narcissism" we find everywhere about us at the end of this century. Lasch described the differences between the two types as follows:

In the classical literature . . . as a psychic formation in which "love rejected turns back to the self as hatred," narcissism has come to be recognized as an important element in the so-called character disorders that have absorbed so much of the clinical attention once given to hysteria and obsessional neurosis. . . . Secondary narcissism, on the other hand, "attempts to annul the pain of disappointed object love" and to nullify the child's rage against those who do not respond immediately to his needs; against those who are now seen to respond to others beside the child and who therefore appear to have abandoned him. . . . The shifting emphasis in clinical studies from primary to secondary narcissism reflects both the shift in psychoanalytical theory from studies of the id to study of the ego and a change in the type of patients seeking psychiatric treatment.[7]

Such "secondary narcissists" are seen as consumed by an "inner rage" at the world, who then "act out" their conflicts instead of repressing and sublimating them:

These patients, though often ingratiating, tend to cultivate a protective shallowness in emotional relations. They lack the capacity to mourn, because the intensity of their rage against lost love objects, in particular against their parents, prevents their reliving happy experiences. . . . Sexually promiscuous rather than repressed, they nevertheless find it impossible to "elaborate the sexual impulse" or to approach sex in the spirit of play. They avoid close involvements, which might release intense feelings of rage. Their personalities consist largely of defenses against this rage and against feelings of oral deprivation.[8]

A little reflection shows that these characteristics do not fit Oedipus. A lack of a capacity to mourn, sexual promiscuity rather than repression, antagonism toward parents, avoidance of close involvements, an overbearing inner rage, and acting out one's inner conflicts instead of sublimating them is not what Oedipus was all about. He clearly did not "lack the capacity to mourn": he grieved greatly at his transgressions, and in his grief (not in his rage!) tore out his eyes. Neither was he sexually promiscuous; indeed, although consorting with his incestuous mother was highly irregular and violated normative proscriptions, he was decidedly chaste, and we are told of no other women in his erotic history. Whether we can consider his behavior "antagonistic toward his parents" is moot. He did not know that

Laius was his father when he killed him on the road. His behavior toward his mother did not "avoid a close involvement." He did not "act out his inner conflicts instead of sublimating them." It is only because he has sublimated them that he gets into trouble in the first place. He does not exhibit symptoms of inner rage. Instead, all his efforts on stage are directed at digging into his own and the city's past, to uncover its and his own secrets. He does this thoughtfully, patiently, and at times, eagerly and excitedly. When he realizes the truth and tears out his eyes, it is acceptance of his guilt; it is expiation, as Paul Fauconnet understood it in *Responsibilité*—the acceptance of responsibility for one's actions, against all odds, and the acceptance of punishment as a penalty to atone for that action. This is quite contrary, of course, to what the Freudian discourse said about him.

Oedipus was one of David Riesman's *inner directed* persons. He had an "internal gyroscope" to which all moral matters were referred, and from which he took his cues for action. The secondary narcissist, as both Sennett and Lasch remind us, moves beyond even other-directedness toward something like an inner-directed condition "except," as Sennett notes, "that in the midst of self-absorption, no one can say what is *inside*," but certainly not the gyroscope typical of a production, rather than a consumption-oriented person.[9]

Thus, the character type that has evolved in this last part of the twentieth century in America is antithetical to Oedipus, and it is not surprising that talk of him has diminished. Oedipus survived the transition in American society from production to consumption, from inner- to other-directedness because the nature of the sexual imagery and the rhetoric of the Freudian vocabulary had become institutionalized. Institutionalized structures are endowed with a variety of inertia and resist efforts at change. But if such efforts persist and are endemic, such verbal structures gradually yield in the face of altered social conditions. With the death of history and the omnivorous thirst for the present, Oedipus, a creature of his own past and of the past of Western culture, has left the stage forever. In his place, still unacknowledged except by inference, has emerged his antithesis, Agamemnon, "that other Greek king," together with his mother-hating daughter Electra, the sociological embodiment of the new era as Oedipus was the psychological embodiment of the earlier one. Agamemnon, the father of Electra, is the personification of the monadic individual imbued with secondary narcissism. In a world rapidly becoming devoid of meaning, he represents the epitome of the new American personality.

It may be tedious, but it is instructive, none-the-less, to review some of the imaginative literature connected with these ancient monarchs whose family trees have dominated Western literary composition for some two thousand years, and the sudden disappearance of one and the appearances on stage of the other in American culture seems to characterize certain cohorts and particular periods. Oedipus has four plays extant, three by Sophocles, *Oedipus the King*, *Antigone*, and *Oedipus at Colonos*; the fourth, by Aeschylus, is *The Seven Against Thebes*, part of another trilogy whose other members have not survived (*Laius* and *Oedipus*). *Oedipus the King* was used by Aristotle in his *Poetics* as the model for tragedy and by Freud for outlining his psychoanalytical method. It describes the methodic discovery of his past on the part of the king. Oedipus had four children by his mother Jocasta, two daughters, Antigone and Ismene, and two sons, Eteocles and Polynices. With the fall of Oedipus, Jocasta's brother Creon ruled Thebes; Oedipus stays on into his old age but becomes an embarrassment to his city and finally leaves with his daughter Antigone. He dies at Colonos, blessing that place with his tomb. That is the situation in *Oedipus at Colonos*. In *The Seven Against Thebes*, his sons fight a civil war, Eteocles becomes king, and the brothers kill each other in battle. Creon decrees that one brother be buried with military honors and the other rot in the sun as a warning to traitors. Antigone rebels at this and openly buries the body of her brother and dooms herself to death as a consequence. This is the theme of *Antigone*.

The saga of Agamemnon is far more extensive. There is, of course, Homer's *Iliad* where he plays a major role, as in all accounts of the Trojan War, he being the commander-in-chief of the Greek forces laying siege to the city. In the *Orestia* of Aeschylus, which won the Athenian tragic competition in 588 B.C., we have a trilogy similar to that of Oedipus: *Agamemnon*, the *Chorephori* (or "Libation Bearers") and the *Eumenides* (or "Graces"). Besides these plays by Aeschylus, Sophocles wrote an

Electra and so did Euripides. Euripides also wrote a play about Agamemnon's son, *Orestes*, and *Iphiginia in Aulis* and *Iphiginia in Tauris*. Iphiginia was Agamemnon's eldest daughter, sacrificed by him to obtain fair winds for the Greek fleet as they sailed to assault Troy. Thus, there are at least twice as many extant Greek plays about the Agamemnon story as there are about the Oedipus tale, and the Agamemnon tale was clearly the favorite among the Greeks and merited the attention of all three great classical playwrights, Aeschylus, Sophocles, and Euripides. The dominant theme in Greek theater is the Agamemnon theme, the House of Atreus, not the House of Laius of Oedipus. This seems to be true of the subsequent theater of the West as well. Shakespeare retells part of the tale in his *Troilus and Cressida* and Eugene O'Neill's trilogy, *Mourning Becomes Electra* (*Homecoming, The Hunted* and *The Haunted*) retells the story in terms of the War Between the States. The theme has attracted the efforts of the major playwrights of the Western world.

We first meet Agamemnon in Homer's *Iliad*, where Homer "sings of Achilles' wrath" on the insult afforded him by Agamemnon, the commander-in-chief of the forces laying siege to Troy. In the opening of the first book of the *Iliad* Agamemnon confronts the priest of Apollo, Chryseis, who seeks the release of his captured daughter, Chryse, and offers a ransom for her to the Greeks. The latter are eager to accept the exchange, "but not so Agamemnon," the Samuel Butler translation tells us: "Agamemnon spoke fiercely to him and sent him roughly away. 'Old man,' said he, 'let me not find you tarrying about our ships, nor coming here hereafter. Your scepter of the god and your wreath shall profit you nothing. I will not free her. She shall grow old in my house at Argos far from her home, busying herself with her loom and visiting my couch. Go, do not provoke me or it shall be the worse for you.' "[10]

This offense to the gods brings down Apollo's wrath on the Greek forces, decimating their ranks with death and plague. When a seer, after seeking the protection of Achilles, the greatest of the Greek warriors, volunteers to testify as to the cause of the plague and cites Agamemnon's affront to Chryseis, Agamemnon "rose in anger. His heart was black with rage and his eyes flashed fire as he scowled and said, 'Seer of evil, you never yet prophesied smooth things concerning me.... and now you come saying Apollo has plagued us because I would not take ransom for the girl, the daughter of Chryseis. I have set my heart on keeping her in my own house, for I love her better than my own wife, Clytemnestra, whose peer she is alike in form and feature, in understanding and accomplishment. However, I will give her up if I must, for I want the people to live, not die. But you must find me another prize to replace her."

The last is an impossible request: the spoils have already been divided, and a captured slave girl prize would have to be taken from some other warrior to replace Agamemnon's loss, something that could not honorably be done. As a consequence, the fight between Achilles and Agamemnon erupts at once, with Achilles characterizing Agamemnon as "covetous beyond all mankind.... steeped in insolence and lust of gain, who always receives the best prizes although others do most of the work!"

Achilles is the king and leader of a Greek force, but Agamemnon is a kind of five-star general, above him in rank. He accordingly orders Achilles to surrender his own girl, Briseis, to him to replace his loss of Chryse. He takes her, and Achilles, his honor offended, sits out the rest of the war. Later, of course, when Agamemnon returns home to Argos he will bring with him neither Chryse nor Briseis, but Cassandra, prophetess daughter of the Trojan king Priam, to further outrage his wife Clytemnestra. So there is a progression of temporary paramours for this arrogant, self-centered, covetous, and insolent king of Argos. His Greek wife, Clytemnestra, is described by the American poet Robinson Jeffers in his narrative poem *The Tower Beyond Tragedy* in wholly negative terms. After noting that Clytemnestra was the sister of Helen, he describes what she was not, rather than what she was, by reminding us of Helen's fabled beauty. Clytemnestra is all Helen was not, he seems to tell us; she was certainly no "burning flower" cut out of stone.

The two brothers, Agamemnon and Menelaus had married two sisters, daughters of Leda (who was wooed by Zeus in the form of a swan), and it was the seduction of the sister Helen, Menelaus's wife, by Paris, son of Priam, the king of Troy, that had set the whole affair going in the first place. It was not the lady's honor at stake, but that of her husband. The offense was not one of seduction but of violation by a guest of his host's hospitality by stealing his host's property, his wife, just as Chryse, Briseis, Cassandra, and by extension Clytemnestra were so much male property.

The reunion of Agamemnon and his Greek wife, Clytemnestra, after the fall of Troy is also described by Jeffers somewhat more graphically than by the Greek playwrights.[11] The scene has a Cecil B. DeMille quality about it: he in his bronze armor clanks up the broad stairs of the palace at Argos with his captives trailing behind him. There are a hundred of the queen's men on each side of his ascent and eighty more on the portico of the palace. As he comes up, Clytemnestra raises her white arms as a signal to her soldiers. They respond by slamming the ends of their spears on the broad flagstones of the porch, and clashing their shields together to raise a furious roar. The scene is reminiscent of the end of the first book of Milton's *Paradise Lost*, where the fallen angels respond to Satan's oath of vengeance on the Almighty for the loss of heaven. At the roaring of the shields wild birds are set loose and shriek across heaven to announce the arrival of the king. Agamemnon looks up and smiles.

His homecoming, in O'Neill's *Mourning Becomes Electra* is less spectacular: Brigadier General Ezra Mannon slips in by night, through the garden, to meet his wife Christine and his daughter Lavinia and son Orin; no slave girl, no trumpets, no assembled troops. It is a guilty return.[12] The guilt we might expect from a moral individual. Agamemnon, on the other hand, carries on his shoulders not only the guilt of his father, Atreus, and that of the sacrifice of Iphiginia, the insult afforded Achilles and the deaths of countless Greeks as a result of his arrogance, but this very arrogance precludes his being conscience stricken or experiencing guilt. In Jeffers's version, the queen describes her husband not unlike the man we find in Homer:

> King Agamemnon,
> My dear, my husband, my lord and yours,
> Is yet not such a man as the gods love;
>   but insolent, fierce, overbearing, whose folly
> Brought many times many great evils

On all the heads and fighting hopes of the Greek
    forces....
Shall I go on and count the other follies of the King?
    The insolence to God and man
That brought down plague, and brought
Achilles' anger against the army?

No, these were too well known, so they are not recounted by
Jeffers. But the stage has been set for Clytemnestra to murder
him in his bath, and murder him she does. The stage directions
for the Aeschylus play tell it all:

(The central doors of the palace open, disclosing Clytemnestra, who
comes forward. She has blood smeared upon her forehead. The body
of Agamemnon lies, muffled in a long robe, within a silver-sided laver;
the corpse of Cassandra is laid beside him.)

Clytemnestra describes how she murdered him:

I trapped him with inextricable toils,
The ill abundance of a baffling robe;
Then smote him, once—again—and at each wound
He cried aloud, then as in death relaxed
Each limb and sank to earth; and as he lay
Once more I smote him, with the third last blow
Sacred to Hades, saviour of the dead.
And thus he fell, and as he passed away
Spirit with body chafed; each dying breath
Flung from his breast swift bubbling jets of gore,
And the dark sprinklings of the rain of blood
Fell upon me.[13]

She rejoices in his death, to the consternation of the Chorus of
city elders. But her joy at his death is short lived, for in the
subsequent plays she will herself be murdered by her daughter
Electra and her son Orestes, a final absolution of the family curse
coming only with *The Eumenides*. Electra hates her mother with
that same vituperative rage against mothers that we find in the
contemporary writing of our narcissistic female monads.[14] Orestes is portrayed by both the Greek playwrights and his latter-
day biographers as weak and dominated by his sister.

The Eumenides or Graces not only absolve Orestes and Electra, but the entire house of its curse. The curse had begun when Atreus and Thyestes, sons of Pelops, became enemies. Thyestes insulted the wife of Atreus (the mother of Agamemnon and Menelaus) and in revenge Atreus seized the children of Thyestes, murdered them, and then cut them up and served them as a meat dish to Thyestes. This crime against the gods originated the curse, which was then passed on to the sons of Atreus. The one son, Agamemnon, kills his daughter, is killed by his wife, and she in turn is killed by her children. Aeschylus finally throws up his hands and transforms the Furies into Graces and offers forgiveness to end the family blood bath.

How well does Agamemnon meet the criteria enunciated for secondary narcissism? If we list these criteria for someone like Oedipus the answer is clear:

Criteria for Secondary Narcissism	Oedipus
1. Lack of capacity to mourn	No
2. Sexual promiscuity rather than repression	No
3. Antagonism toward parents	No
4. Avoidance of Close Involvements	No
5. Overbearing inner rage	No
6. Acting out inner conflicts, not sublimating them	No

Oedipus clearly does not fit the narcissistic monad of the close of the century: he scores No on all the criteria. On the other hand, if we apply these same criteria to Agamemnon we obtain very different results; as a matter of fact, the opposite results. Agamemnon does indeed lack the capacity to mourn: he does not mourn the death of Iphiginea, his daughter, whom he sacrificed to obtain fair winds for the fleet to set sail for Troy; Clytemnestra mourns her many years later, but Agamemnon never discusses her. Indeed, he appears unable to experience any form of guilt, and as Achilles reminds us in the *Iliad*, Agamemnon does not think twice of taking the best of everything for himself, even to the detriment of his colleagues and the increased risk to their joint enterprise. His sexual promiscuity is blatant: Clytemnestra, Briseis and Chryse, Cassandra and

Cressida, and probably others. It is not incidental that Clytemnestra murders his current mistress, Cassandra. Sexual repression and deferred gratification seem foreign to him. He avoids close involvements with all these women and with the male members of the host besieging Troy; Agamemnon has no friends, unlike the other heroes at camp. Achilles has Patroclus, for example. Agamemnon's inner rage continually overflows, as in the quotations above drawn from Homer and the descriptions of him by his wife. He speaks fiercely, even to the peaceful priest of Apollo, and bullies the weak. He is "insolent, fierce, overbearing," and his follies bring down "great evils" upon others. He sublimates nothing, acting out whatever inner conflicts he has, a thoroughly disagreeable, self-centered (and familiar) personality.

If we compare his scoring with that of Oedipus, the only criterion presenting difficulty is point number 3, "Antagonism Toward Parents." We lack evidence on this score, although he is frequently referred to in the Greek texts as a "son of Atreus" and the sin of Atreus was well known not only to the audiences of the Athenian theater, but presumably to the other characters of Homer's epic. In the Aeschylus play (and in Jeffers's modern poem) his wife, Clytemnestra, has taken on Thyeste's only uneaten son, Aegisthus, as her lover in Agamemnon's absence. Although Agamemnon acknowledges that this is his nephew, no mention is made of the original sin committed by his father against his uncle. His character seems so resistant to guilt that he is effectively isolated from any verbal expression of the guilt besetting his house and its descendants.

The biography of Agamemnon and the analysis above indicates clearly that Agamemnon is the archetype of the contemporary monad we find everywhere about us at the end of the twentieth century. It appears that Oedipus did "not go gentle into that good night," but was shoved off the stage by the arrogant Agamemnon, hungry to not only have it all, but to have it all *now* at all costs. There are, of course, other reasons for characterizing the end of the American century as the Age of Agamemnon: the much heralded Age of Aquarius never arrived, subverted by the eclipse of Oedipus and the fracturing of meanings. In addition, much feminist rhetoric has an Electra rather than an Antigone ring to it: the daughter figure has changed. Antigone risked death on her brother's behalf, something unthinkable of Electra. And many young men seem Orestian, unable to perform without the prodding of their sisters. The heightened antagonism between the sexes is foreign to the Oedipus story, but ever present in the saga of Agamemnon, as it is today. Finding oneself in an anomic society where the normative has lost its obligatory persuasiveness and meanings not only are held in abeyance[15] but rapidly disappear as meaning itself becomes less salient, the "monads with gonads" that are produced exploit each other for their own instant gratification and are unwilling or unable to contemplate anything of value that does not relate directly to themselves.

Oedipus was a man who sought meanings. He owed his status in Thebes not to lineage—no one knew he was the son of Laius—but to his uncanny ability in deciphering the riddle of the sphinx, in discovering her meaning. His inquiring mind led him to solve another problem, the murder on the highway. He searched within himself for the elements of meaning regarding his own history, and in doing so he went too far and destroyed himself by the subsequent revelation. It was the king's search for meaning that Freud found as the key for establishing psychoanalytical theory. Meanings are intrinsic to the Oedipus legend. This is true not only of the actions of the King, but of his daughter Antigone as well. They are moral persons caught in the web of circumstance and history. The resurrected Oedipus of the first half of the twentieth century died later in the century with the death of meanings, and of meaning. He became irrelevant in the context of the narcissistic monads who then took the stage.

Agamemnon was, as Jeffers tells us, a man not loved by the gods: insolent, blind to the needs of others, particularly blind to their needs for honor, virtue, respect, inviolability: all the altruisms, all the high-sounding ideas that strive to signify that the individual has a need to live in a world populated by others, a world peopled by more than a solitary self. His daughter Electra has nothing in common with Antigone, the heroic daughter of Oedipus. Agamemnon became the chief executive officer of the major enterprise of his day by denying charity to others and imposing his own immediate appetites and willfulness upon his fellows, particularly upon those who were not in positions to either resist or fight back—slaves, women, underlings, religious leaders, and the weak and the powerless of the Greek city states. Achilles, after all, was an exception: the great hero who embodied all the virtues of his world as Agamemnon embodied all its failings and liabilities. Achilles was godlike because he was the grandson of Zeus himself, was championed by Apollo, god of beauty and reason. The best Achilles could do was to sulk in his tent and pout like a child, powerless in his mortification at the offense done to his manhood, overwhelmed not so much by the insult offered him by Agamemnon as by the knowledge that, to Agamemnon, the offense was trivial, inconsequential, so long as his own immediate appetite was gratified.

Although the culture of present-day America has become increasingly narcissistic, as Lasch insists, it is perhaps wrong to characterize it as the Culture of Narcissism, as he has done. It is a misnomer. Narcissis, after all, was a pretty Greek lad who sat on a rock by a pool admiring his reflection in the water—like the nymph in the White Rock ginger ale advertisements. It is not this pretty Greek boy who characterizes the emerging culture of our time. It is Agamemnon, and with him, his daughter Electra; in our time, the female has gained prominence with the male. In our time, these are the alien strangers who walk across our stage.

NOTES

1. Michel Foucault has published several volumes loosely grouped together as *The History of Sexuality*. His first book with that title appears in English as Volume I: *Introduction*, published by Vintage Books, a division of Random House, in 1980 and available in paper. This was followed by Volume Two, with the title, *The Use of Pleasure* by the same publisher in 1986. Volume Three, *Care of the Self*, was issued by Pantheon Books in hardcover only in 1986. In addition the book *Herculine Barbin: Being the Recently Discovered Memoirs of a Nineteenth-Century French Hermaphrodite*, edited and with an introduction by Foucault, should be included in this series. It was published in English in 1980 by Pantheon.

2. See Paul Fouconnet, *La Responsibilité* (Paris: Alcan), 1928. Fouconnet was a student of Durkheim and active in the *L'Année* enterprise.

3. David Riesman, Nathan Glazer and Reuel Denny, *The Lonely*

Crowd: A Study in the Changing American Character (New Haven: Yale University Press), 1950.

4. Christopher Lasch, *The Culture of Narcissism: American Life in an Age of Diminishing Expectations*. (New York: Warner Books), 1979. See also his *Haven in a Heartless World: The Family Besieged* (New York: Basic Books), 1977.

5. Joel Kovel, *A Complete Guide to Therapy* (New York: Random House), 1978, 8.

6. Richard Sennet, *The Fall of Public Man* (New York: Random House), 1978, 8.

7. Lasch, 1979, 79–80.

8. Lasch, 1979, 81.

9. Sennet, 1978, 5.

10. Homer, the *Iliad*. Translated by Samuel Butler (New York: Black), 1942, 8.

11. Robinson Jeffers, *Roan Stallion, Tamar and Other Poems* (New York: Modern Library), 1935, 23.

12. Eugene O'Neill, *Nine Plays* (New York: Modern Library), 1932.

13. Whitney Oates and Eugene O'Neill, Jr. (eds.), *The Complete Greek Drama*. Vol. 1 (New York: Random House), 1938.

14. See, for example, Nancy Friday, *My Mother, My Self* (New York: Dell), 1977.

15. Durkheim, in his classic work *Suicide*, notes that in times of anomie, the classification of men and things is suspended, and "time is required for the collective conscience to reclassify them." But a collective conscience of the variety envisioned by Durkheim is no longer possible, although there occur frantic attempts at artificially creating them. The collective conscience depends upon a web of association, an interconnection among and between individuals that is suffused with mutually understood meanings. But as I have attempted to show in this book and elsewhere, such shared understanding has largely disappeared and a meaningful bond can no longer be established between two people that is enduring, as each is trapped in the narcissistic concerns of his and her own passionless self-contemplation devoid of anything but relativistic values.

Chapter 13

Is Society Possible?

Meanings lie in the relations among things, and the relation among things reflects the relations among people, "among men," as Durkheim and Mauss phrased it earlier in this century. "The relations among men determines the relations among things." It was Ferdinand de Saussure who pointed out to us that in language, words do not point to things, nor are they substitutes for things. Words point to other words, and it is the relationships between words that determines the meanings encoded and manifested by language. Only a member of a speech community can understand what is being said or written within that community because the member knows the rules governing the order of words in sentences and the paradigmatic sets of bits of meanings that exist in and around particular sounds in that language.

Relations among humans determine the relations among things. Relations among words determine the meanings in language. Language is the semiotic system by means of which we seek to examine the relations among things, their meanings. Meanings lie in relations. As relations disintegrate, meanings disintegrate. The existentialist protests of the post-World War II period sought to place the ontological problem, the problem of *beingness*, prior to the epistemological problem, the problem of *meaning*. At the close of the twentieth century, it appears that the ontological has at last taken precedence: meanings have been suffocated by a preoccupation with being. The omnipresent Now and the dismissal of deferred gratification of libidinous appetites has rendered questions of meaning irrelevant. In the earlier chapters of this book meanings have been shown to be disappearing or already to have disappeared, in the empirical cases discussed. Meaning itself fades away. The relations among things and the relations among people have been made increasingly problematic. Today the question may not be asked, What is the relation among men? In its place is the question, What is the relation among groups? Groups, however, are things, concepts, not quite the same as the individual. Democracy championed the equality of each individual under the law, not privilege for an individual as a consequence of his or her membership in a particular group, whatever that group's history in a past where the current individual did not exist. The decline of democracy under increasing authoritarianism calls for inequality under the law, favored treatment of some individuals over other individuals. The Nazis championed this approach in favoring aryans over Jews, gypsies, Poles, and Freemasons. Nationalism, which takes to itself a special chosen group of people, is becoming the principal enemy of democracy. In the de-sovietized, de-socialist nations of the Balkans group loyalty parading itself as nationalism has evoked wholesale slaughter and rapes not only in Yugoslavia but in other Balkan areas and previous Soviet republics. Inequality under the law is being sought throughout the West. The Serbs consider the Croats lesser people than themselves, as the Germans did their Jewish citizens, as the Israelis do their Arab citizens. Relations among men deteriorate as relations among words deteriorate. But the opposite is also true: as relations among men deteriorate, the relations among words deteriorate with them, and meaning is lost.

In American society the "yuppies" of the past decade have lost their battle: living costs became too high, the cost of housing out of reach, the electronic gear unsatisfying and too expensive anyway; one could not "have it all," after all. It became a meaningless pursuit. Unable to find meaningful relations with other individuals, the yuppy had sought to find meanings in inanimate things, unaware that the first determined the second: if one finds no meanings in persons, one is certain to find no meanings in things. Their attempts to form relationships with at least one other person either through marriage or connubiation clearly did not work: divorce rates soared and the length of marriages shrank with the shriveling length of relationships. If the birth rate fell, it was because children too were seen as meaningless: they cost money that might otherwise be used for acquiring material possessions and required a kind of lifelong commitment that seemed unthinkable. Unable to make a lifelong commitment to a mate, why bother to make one to an unknown child? The unborn remained unborn, or, if accidental pregnancy occurred, were readily aborted. Abortion rates soared. "What's love got to do with it?" became not only the lyrics of a popular song, but a way of life. Love demands the kind of commitment to a long-term relationship with another that suddenly seemed devoid of meaning. How had such things been possible in the past? the emerging monads asked. The answer was simple: their parents and others of the past simply didn't know any better.

The emergence of the self-centered, asocial monad, replacing the social dyads and triads of earlier times, the ego-focused, Now-focused, omnivorous devourer of anything providing stimulation, went hardly noticed at first. It was not simply visual and sexual stimulation and gratification that was championed, although such things as masturbation and sado-masochistic practices and shops selling the required videos and illustrated "manuals" centered on the self were suddenly championed. The market exploded with a million and one new foods, gadgets, clothes—commodities of all kinds. The media catered to all these tendencies and helped accelerate them. New self-styled experts came into existence; the Surgeon General descended Capitol Hill like a bearded prophet to make pronouncements on the evils of tobacco, the virtues of condoms, the pseudoscientific therapeutics of oat bran and similar dietary fads. The yogurt eaters multiplied. People were encouraged to jog, then to run. New business opportunities were quickly seized upon; the virtues of aerobic exercises had untold numbers of women bobbing up and down, clapping their hands, and destroying their arches to newly taped commercial videos. The coupling of erotic images of males and females in minimal spandex-tight clothing exercising together in spas and gyms helped create additional business opportunities. Cereal promotions were aimed at adults instead of children, and the proliferation of "feminine products" of an infinite variety were all promoted by TV images and magazine illustrations, probing the most intimate details of female anatomy and insecurity.

The monads multiplied, and, in their jogging, aerobic exercising, and "nontraditional" "back-to-college" adventures sought to find the meanings otherwise lacking in their lives. They quickly learned that they could not find meaning in casual sexual activity, and the emergence of AIDS began to make discouraging inroads on such efforts anyway. Unable to find or make a "meaningful relationship" in the absence of meaning, the level of their frustration increased. It is a truism of the social sciences, perhaps its only truism, that frustration leads to aggression. Aggression takes many forms. The inner rage of Lasch's narcissist is one form of it. This leads to resentment of the parents, especially the mothers. But it also leads to a propensity to blame others for one's own lack of success, of achievement, of "having it all." One begins to see oneself as victimized: not personally perhaps, not directly, but indirectly because one is a member of a group and, one claims, that group has been victimized. The demand for special treatment Now to correct injustices done to one's group in the past becomes the norm, not just for blacks, for women, American Indians, Latinos, gays and lesbians, but even on behalf of wordless animals: whales and baby seals become the martyrs of a new religion. With the disappearance of meanings ideologies come into existence to support any and all possible positions that might accrue benefits to the members of groups now demanding special treatment, now contending with other groups to dominate the definition of social situations.

The demise of holidays, their conflation into sameness instead of difference; the routinization of applause; the increased efforts at defusing meaning from articulations; the increased use of icons, images, pictures, and non-language symbols to replace the possibility of meanings encoded in verbal language; the maimed messages; politically controlled flow of information; the deconstruction of texts and demands for "politically correct" uniformity on college campuses, grade inflation and the weakening of requirements for advanced degrees—all these point to the death of meaning. If, as French social commentators first taught us, Man is dead, the humanistic enterprise gone, the impersonal global multinational corporations determining what is possible to do or not do, then the death of Man is a consequence of the death of meaning. We can no longer define ourselves if the possibility of definition lies in the relation among words and if what these words seek to elucidate is the relation among things determined by the relations among us.

We can summarize the processes involved in the empirical data of the above and in the previous chapters as follows:

1. *Iconization.* The movement from the language of words to manipulation of the consciousness by selected images: the decline of newspapers; the flowering of TV, movies, videos, picture textbooks; Apple and Macintosh computers; and Windows programs, and DOS conversion to icons. This movement away from demotic language to picture language reverses the long historical trend.

2. *Routinization.* The substitution of one response for the variety of responses previously demanded by the differences in meaning. This promotes the deletion of assigned meanings. The expansion of the use of applause is an example.

3. *Equalization.* The removal of differences in meaning between and among elements by equating the elements. The substitution typical of routinization need not be involved in equalization. The equating of "sexism" with "racism" is one such equalization.

4. *Defusing.* The dismissal of the proffered or intended meaning in favor of one more acceptable to the defusing respondent, an interactional phenomenon at the individual level.

5. *Redefinition.* As in 4, but by a group competing for domination of definitions of social situations favorable to itself.

6. *Cathecticazation.* Redundant use of highly charged, emotionally persuasive words to circumvent rational explanation.

7. *Information Control.* Efforts by government and commercial interests as well as by competing groups to limit available vocabulary, syntax, and narrative.

8. *Censorship.* Increased efforts to preclude the publication or limit the distribution of textual materials deemed unacceptable by one of the competing groups. This includes demands to change language in

textbooks, eliminate pornography, prevent the sale of phonograph records, and limit library acquisitions of books deemed objectionable by national, racial, religious, ethnic, or women's groups.

9. *Currency.* Attempts to obliterate meanings by appealing to the current date or decade, as, for example, "After all, this is the 1990s," as if currency automatically confers some new truth content upon situations or things. The myth of progress here is assigned to the calendar.

This listing, although by no means comprehensive, allows us a glimpse of the processes at work in destroying meaning.

It was the English philosopher Thomas Hobbes who first raised the question, "How is society possible?" It was Georg Simmel, the German sociologist who, perhaps very much ahead of his time early in this century, raised it again. For Simmel, the eighteenth century had witnessed the struggle for political equality and freedom. By the nineteenth century individuals wanted to be "different" from each other: in the Romantic era this "difference" became paramount. Simmel saw the ensuing struggle between these two opposing motivations as "western Man's spiritual struggle" for self-definition. How can one be both equal to others but simultaneously be different? In twentieth-century America this reached a crisis with respect to education that was resolved by the courts: equal but separate educational facilities were discontinued as harboring an implicit contradiction. By separating black students from white students one could not provide "equal" treatment, for one was creating another inequality. Desegregation of schools was accordingly demanded and became widespread, and integration became the ultimate goal. But as the black journalist Shelby Steele noted, the dream of integration envisioned in the 1960s has largely disappeared, and willful separation into competing groups has replaced it. Groups are demanding not equal treatment, but special treatment, for their members. Campuses throughout the nation have become fractured by the isolation of these groups, one from another, and their clamorous demands for greater shares of the resources. The narcissism of their egoistic demands is revealed in even casual encounters.

As this activity proliferates, meanings increasingly disappear and we seek solutions in arcane practices, abandoned techniques. A new puritanism emerges which, pretending to espouse personal freedom, preoccupies itself with the sensational and salacious, capitalizes in the media upon each happening that contains possibly sexual overtones or implications. Oedipal guilt yields to Agamemnon's aggression. Prominent personalities in the popular culture appear on TV programs and in magazines and describe how they were sexually molested as children; rape stories, true or false, are eagerly seized upon. Where an earlier and guilty Puritanism sought immortality of the soul, the new guiltless puritanism seeks immortality of the body. Untoward activity toward the body is therefore abhorred. Smoking, for example, becomes the new cardinal sin. Exercise becomes the new exorcism. Daily revelations in the media proclaim new dietary threats, new medical procedures, new cosmetic appliances. The body becomes the central preoccupation of the new puritans. The testimony of children regarding molestation mirrors the testimony of the girls at Salem in the earlier Puritanism. Entire nursery schools are dismembered across the nation on the testimony of children who, in jurisprudence, are not legally able to furnish such testimony. People ignorant of history voice demands to "take back the night," not realizing that we never had it, that the nighttime streets were never the province of the law-abiding citizen, but always belonged to the night people, a marginal population in western societies.

Whether society is possible under these conditions remains to be seen. It is clear that the social system cannot meet unlimited demands upon it: resources given to some must be taken from others. The demands for equality too often mask demands for exclusivity and privilege. Blame cannot be placed indiscriminately upon others without accepting some of the "blame" oneself. Societies have existed because of mutually understood rules governing give and take; one must give as well as take. John F. Kennedy's inaugural maxim may seem trite, but it was none the less meaningful at the time.

Sociologists can analyze social conditions with the theoretical tools at their disposal, but must never be trusted with offering cures for perceived errors or wrongs. That is the duty of the politician operating under the rule of law. If, at the end of the century, Americans are expressing an increased hostility to their politicians, it is because politicians have lost sight of what society is all about and their responsibility to help maintain it, even if it is to the detriment of business, industry and the military. If Man is dead, as the Europeans tell us, then Man must be resurrected, even if this means at the expense of the economy. The great humanist insistence on the worth and dignity of the human individual must be reasserted, and equal treatment under the law renewed.

Bibliography

Barthes, Roland. *Writing, Degree Zero and the Elements of Semiology*. Boston: Beacon Press, 1968.

———. *The Pleasure of the Text*. New York: Hill and Wang, 1975.

Becker, Ernest. *The Denial of Death*. New York: Free Press, 1973.

Bellah, Robert. *The Broken Covenant*. New York: Seabury, 1975.

Bull, Malcolm. 1989. "Seventh Day Adventists: Heretics of American Civil Religion." *Sociological Analysis* 50(2), 177–187.

Connor, Steven. *Postmodern Culture: An Introduction to Theories of the Contemporary*. Oxford: Basil Blackwell, 1989.

Derrida, Jacques. *Of Grammatology*. Baltimore: Johns Hopkins University Press, 1976.

Douglas, Mary. *Implicit Meanings*. London: Routledge and Kegan Paul, 1975.

Durkheim, Emile. *Rules of the Sociological Method*. New York: Free Press, 1938.

———. *The Elementary Forms of the Religious Life*. New York: Free Press, 1969.

Durkheim, Emile, and Marcel Mauss. *Primitive Classification*. Chicago: University of Chicago Press, 1963.

Eliade, Mircea. *The Sacred and the Profane*. New York: Harcourt Brace and Jovanovich, 1959.

Erikson, Kai T. *Everything in its Path*. New York: Simon and Schuster, 1976.

Festinger, Leon, H. W. Riecken, and S. Schachter. *When Prophecy Fails.* Minneapolis: University of Minnesota Press, 1956.

Foucault, Michel. "Discourse on Language," included as an appendix in *The Archaeology of Knowledge.* New York: Harper and Row, 1972.

————. *Introduction.* Vol. 1, *The History of Sexuality.* New York: Vintage, 1980.

————. *The Use of Pleasure.* Vol. 2, *The History of Sexuality.* New York: Vintage, 1986.

————. *Care of the Self.* Vol. 3, *The History of Sexuality.* New York: Pantheon, 1986.

Fouconnet, Paul. *La Responsibilité.* Paris: Alcan, 1928.

Friday, Nancy. *My Mother, My Self.* New York: Dell, 1977.

Garfinkle, Harold. *Studies in Ethnomethodology.* Englewood Cliffs, NJ: Prentice-Hall, 1967.

Goffman, Erving. *The Presentation of Self in Everyday Life.* New York, Anchor, 1959.

Halio, Marcia Peoples. January 1990. "Student writing: Can the Machine Maim the Message?" *Academic Computing,* 17.

Hesse, Hermann. *Steppenwolf.* New York: Bantam, 1969.

Hirsch, E. D., Jr. *Cultural Literacy: What Every American Needs to Know.* Boston: Houghton Mifflin, 1987.

Jeffers, Robinson. *Roan Stallion, Tamar and Other Poems.* New York: Modern Library, 1935.

Kovel, Joel. *A Complete Guide to Therapy.* New York: Random House, 1978.

Lasch, Christopher. *Haven in a Heartless World: The Family Besieged.* New York, Basic Books, 1977.

————. *The Culture of Narcissism: American Life in an Age of Diminishing Expectations.* New York: Warner Books, 1979.

Leifer, Ron. *In the Name of Mental Health: The Social Functions of Psychiatry.* New York: Science House, 1969.

Lemert, Charles. *Sociology and the Twilight of Man.* Carbondale, Ill.: Southern Illinois University Press, 1979.

Levine, Donald. *Georg Simmel: On Sociability and Social Forms.* Chicago: University of Chicago Press, 1971.

Levi-Strauss, Claude. *Structural Anthropology.* New York: Basic Books, 1963.

Luhmann, Niklas. *Love as Passion.* Cambridge, Mass.: Harvard University Press, 1986.

————. *Ecological Communication.* Chicago: University of Chicago Press, 1989.

Lukes, Steven. *Emile Durkheim, His Life and Work*. Middlesex: Penguin Books, 1973.

Lyman, Stanford, and Marvin Scott. 1969. "Accounts." *American Sociological Review*, 33, 46–63.

Lyotard, Jean-François. *The Postmodern Condition*. Manchester: Manchester University Press, 1984.

Mannheim, Karl. *Ideology and Utopia*. New York: Harcourt Brace and Ward, 1939.

Martin, David. *A General Theory of Secularization*. New York: Harper and Row, 1979.

Merton, Robert K. *Science and Technology in Seventeenth Century England*. New York: Harper and Row, 1970.

Molotch, Harvey L., and Deidre Boden. 1985. "Talking Social Structure: Discourse, Domination and the Watergate Hearings." *American Sociological Review* 50, 273–287.

Nisbet, Robert. *History of the Idea of Progress*. New York: Basic Books, 1980.

Oates, Whitney, and Eugene O'Neill, Jr. (eds.). *The Complete Greek Drama*. Vol. 1. New York: Random House, 1938.

O'Neill, Eugene. *Nine Plays*. New York: Modern Library, 1932.

Paglia, Camille. *Sexual Personae: Art and Decadence from Nerfertiti to Emily Dickinson*. New York: Vintage, 1991.

Riesman, David, Nathan Glazer, and Reuel Denny. *The Lonely Crowd: A Study in the Changing American Character*. New Haven: Yale University Press, 1950.

Sacks, Harvey. "An Initial Investigation of the Usability of Conversational Data." In D. Sudnow, *Studies in Interaction*. New York: Free Press, 1972.

de Saussure, Ferdinand. *Course in General Linguistics*. New York: McGraw-Hill, 1959.

Schlosstein, Steven. *The End of the American Century*. Chicago: Congdon and Weed, 1989.

Seidman, Steven. *Romantic Longings: Love in America, 1830–1980*. New York: Routledge, 1991.

Sennett, Richard. *The Fall of Public Man*. New York: Random House, 1978.

Steele, Shelby. 1992. "The New Sovereignty." *Harper's*, 285 (1706).

Szasz, Thomas. *The Myth of Mental Illness*. New York: Harper and Row, 1961.

Tannen, Deborah. *You Just Don't Understand: Women and Men in Conversation*. New York: William Morrow and Company, 1990.

Wallwork, Ernest. *Durkheim: Morality and Milieu*. Cambridge, Mass.: Harvard University Press, 1972.

Weber, Max. *The Sociology of Religion*. Boston: Beacon Press, 1963.

Zito, George V. 1983. "Toward a Sociology of Heresy." *Sociological Analysis* 44(2), 123–130.

———. *Systems of Discourse: Structures and Semiotics in the Social Sciences*. Westport, Conn.: Greenwood Press, 1984.

———. *The Sociology of Shakespeare*. New York: Peter Lang, 1991.

Index

About the Author

GEORGE V. ZITO is Associate Professor of Sociology at Syracuse University. He is the author of seven books, including *Systems of Discourse* (Greenwood, 1984) and *The Sociology of Shakespeare* (1991).